Killer Bodybuilder Kelly Ann Ryan

Ana Benson

Published by Trellis Publishing, 2021.

While every precaution has been taken in the preparation of this book, the publisher assumes no responsibility for errors or omissions, or for damages resulting from the use of the information contained herein.

KILLER BODYBUILDER KELLY ANN RYAN

First edition. July 1, 2021.

Copyright © 2021 Ana Benson.

ISBN: 979-8223837367

Written by Ana Benson.

KILLER BODYBUILDER

KELLY ANN RYAN

2

ANA BENSON

The world of professional bodybuilding is interesting and intriguing. It is more than just strong and muscular bodies. As a matter of fact, there are many hidden aspects of it which include the use of steroids and other dangerous substances. Kelly Ann Ryan was an all-American girl who started out as a gymnast trained by Béla Károlyi. Her interest in the sport led her to a very successful bodybuilding career.

She met her future husband in 1999 and the two of them quickly became the power couple in the world of fitness. But all of their dreams will come crashing down in 2005 after a jealously fueled evening in their Las Vegas mansion that led to the death of their assistant Melissa James.

Early life

Kelly Ann Ryan was born on 10th of July 1972 in Minneapolis, Minnesota but she grew up in Greenville, South Carolina. She was always an active child who loved sports, so it comes as no surprise to discover she got interested in gymnastics at the age of eight. Her passion for physical activities will help her later in life because it became the basis of everything she did. As soon as she started high school, she signed herself up for the cheerleading squad and was the one who came up with choreographies for the entire team. Not to forget that she was also interested in basketball.

Gymnastics and dance were her two passions and she dreamed of becoming a professional cheerleader, dancing for one of major basketball teams that played in the NBA. As a matter of fact, Kelly Ann wanted to become a Lakers girl. She got accepted to the University of South Carolina after finishing high school and Kelly Ann majored in journalism. She earned her money working as a choreographer back then and still planned to move to Los Angeles when she got her degree in journalism. But one day she saw women's fitness competition broadcasted on the television and Kelly Ann was mesmerized. The women who were parading on the stage were gorgeous and strong which appealed to her right away. She knew that her training and self-discipline could get her up there, so her new goal was to sign up for a fitness competition as soon as possible.

Kelly Ann's first fitness competition was NPC South Carolina State back in 1995. Her performance was unique because it combined everything she was good at – dance and gymnastics. Kelly Ann was a breeze of fresh air that left an impression on the judges, so she got the number one spot. It was clear that there was something unique about this girl and everyone wanted to see more. Plus, she earned a catchy nickname after her first stage appearance – The Flying Ryan. Kelly Ann continued training and attending various fitness competitions, and that is where she met Craig Titus in 1999.

Craig had a bad reputation within the fitness community mostly because he cultivated the angry and untouchable stage persona. He was interested in Kelly Ann from the moment he saw her on stage in Panama Beach competition, but she dismissed him right away. Craig was stubborn and continued to invite her on dates until she finally said yes. But Craig wasn't as squeaky clean as Kelly Ann assumed. As a matter of fact, he was arrested for possession with the intent to sell back in 1995. The police found ecstasy tablets on him during a routine search. However, he wasn't locked up and got away with a probation which allowed him to continue to compete. But he tested positive for steroids which earned him a temporary ban.

His bad boy persona was confirmed in 1997 when he failed his obligatory drug test which was a part of the probation. Craig had opiates on him so he ended up spending twenty-one months in a federal prison. It is a guarded facility that is stricter than a standard prison. Craig Titus was always open about his use of steroids and that topic was quite familiar to anyone involved in the highly competitive world of fitness. Building muscle is hard and forbidden substances are a part of it. The ban wasn't an obstacle for Craig and he worked really hard to return to the stage and shine once again. He also did his best to win Kelly Ann over because he did fall for her. Eventually, she agreed to go on a date with him, and she was enchanted by his honesty and determination. The two were very much in love by the end of the 1990s.

The couple moved to Las Vegas in 2000 and they got married in July of the same year. Las Vegas already had an established bodybuilding scene so Craig and Kelly Ann quickly found work. After all, they were quite famous in those circles, and everyone knew who they were. Kelly Ann became a personal coach and had numerous endorsement deals. They were making a lot of money by doing appearances to various bodybuilding events. Kelly Ann's appearance fee was somewhere between $2500 and $3000. The couple got wealthy in a short period of time, so they purchased a large mansion which had its own private gym, a movie theater, and three garages. They would also spend a lot of money on expensive cars. Kelly Ann was especially proud of her red Jaguar which was truly an eye-catching vehicle. Since Las Vegas is the city of endless parties, it comes as no surprise that the couple was known for wild celebrations every time they won a competition. These parties were often filled with drugs and opiates. The attendees would use cocaine, meth, OxyContin, etc.

Meeting Melissa James

Craig and Kelly Ann knew how to market themselves so they had a seemingly endless income. They were sponsored by many famous brands and were always looking for job opportunities. Craig appeared on more than a hundred front pages by various fitness magazines. Since they were so busy all the time, Kelly Ann and Craig made a decision to hire a personal assistant that would help them out. They selected Melissa James who was a Florida-based dancer, and was interested in the bodybuilding community. She was also their longtime friend. Melissa had a similar upbringing as Kelly Ann - she came from a small town and wanted to find success on the West Coast. She met Craig at a bodybuilding competition in Panama Beach back in 1999 and the two remained in contact. Craig later revealed that he had a short affair with Melissa at that event and that he personally invited her to come to Las Vegas. As he put it, Melissa wanted to be a well-known dancer, and he knew that there will be more opportunities for her in Las Vegas.

While Melissa was a bit on a fence about moving her entire life to Las Vegas, she did think about it a lot. Eventually, she was invited to work on an exercise program, namely to choreograph the moves. The job took her to Las Vegas, and she fell in love with the city right away. It was a breathtaking place and she soon started coming back more often. Melissa was spending more time with Craig and Kelly Ann and helped them out with several business projects. They saw how capable she was, so she became their live-in assistant in the beginning of 2005. Melissa's dance studio which was located in Florida was closed down and she had nothing else going on at the moment.

Kelly Ann and Craig were planning to open a store and they needed someone to sort everything out. Craig would later say that Kelly Ann knew about his relationship with Melissa which was happening during the time she lived with them and that his wife willingly participated in threesomes with Melissa and Craig. But the love triangle was a very dangerous thing, especially with all things considered. There was an additional aspect of Las Vegas which Melissa enjoyed, and that was the party scene. She wasn't a stranger to party drugs and other opiates which were consumed at the bashes thrown by her bosses. As a matter of fact, their lavish events were well-known throughout the city because they often involved orgies and lots of narcotics.

The discovery of Melissa James' remains

In the early hours of December 14th, 2005, the Las Vegas Police Department got a call from a truck driver who was on a highway outside of the city. He reported seeing two speeding cars which flew by his vehicle. They got off the road and the truck driver noticed a fire in the distance, seemingly somewhere in the desert. The driver also saw a gray pickup truck coming from the same direction and it seemed suspicious to him because only one vehicle returned to the road. The fire department got to the scene of the arson, and they were shocked to find out that an expensive red Jaguar was set on fire. They were used to dealing with people burning old or unwanted vehicles in the desert, so the chief thought that this was just a standard case when they received the call.

The car itself was clearly torched on purpose and left there to burn out. The chief was checking out the remains of the car when he saw a red jacket and something resembling a human arm poking out from under the back seat. After a closer inspection, he realized that it was a body lying in the trunk. The fire department contacted the police right away and the officers who responded first were horrified by what they were seeing. It was almost impossible to determine the gender of the charred remains, but they thought it might be a female due to the style of a jacket and the bracelets which were found on the corpse.

They quickly ran the car through the database and determined that the owner was Kelly Ann Ryan. The first assumption was that she was the corpse in the trunk. A police car drove up to her address expecting to find Craig Titus alone in the house. But when they rang the doorbell and Kelly Ann came up to greet them, the police officers were slightly confused. Kelly Ann looked like she was expecting them and told the officers that her car was stolen last night while she slept. She provided them with more information than they really needed which set off the alarm right away.

Her story was that she went to bed early and once she got up, her red Jaguar was gone. Kelly Ann immediately told them that she suspected that her live-in assistant Melissa James was the thief because apparently Craig and Kelly Ann found out that Melissa was doing drugs and they threw her out of the house immediately. But since they were fond of her, the couple rented a room for Melissa in one of Las Vegas hotels and bought her a plane ticket back home. The law enforcement who spoke to Kelly Ann was left baffled by all this data. They wrote down Melissa's name but were unsure about the method of identifying the remains from the trunk because the hands were badly burned. There will be no way of determining if the body was indeed Melissa off the fingerprints alone. But there was always DNA testing.

The officers went through Kelly Ann's and Craig's garage but couldn't find the gray pickup truck either. A similar vehicle wasn't registered to either of them so they quickly realized that might be the missing puzzle piece which will tell them everything they needed to know about the crime which occurred during the early hours of December 14th. They returned to the station hoping that the medical examiner had more information about the corpse. When the body was delivered to the coroner's office, the personnel noticed that the entire head was wrapped in duct tape. Once they peeled it off, the medical examiner was shocked to find out that the face was untouched by fire. It was in contrast to the rest of the corpse which was pretty much unrecognizable. The police officers found Melissa's picture and compared it to the face preserved by the tape – it was a match.

Back in Florida, Melissa James' mother was waiting for her daughter at the airport but she never arrived. She knew where Melissa was staying while she was in Las Vegas so she called Craig's and Kelly Ann's mansion. Nobody was picking up the phone, so she got really worried, dreading that something bad might have happened to all three of them. But the Las Vegas Police Department has already called up Melissa's father and told him that his daughter might be dead. They needed a DNA sample to confirm that information. Melissa's mother immediately set off to Las Vegas to help with the investigation.

Melissa's body was in horrible condition so finding out the real cause of death was a real challenge to the medical examiner. After running a toxicology test, they did find a high dosage of opiates in her system. However, they couldn't confirm that Melissa died of an overdose. They also saw bruises around her neck which suggested that she was strangled as well. The rest of her body was burned so there was a possibility that there were more wounds which were covered up. It was clear that something violent happened to Melissa and the police investigation had to start somewhere. Kelly Ann's and Craig's story was weak and since they were the ones who last saw Melissa alive, the detectives were sure that there was more to the story.

The investigation and the hunt

Melissa's mother was completely devastated by the death of her daughter. She wanted to help the police identify the killer as soon as possible. The investigators questioned her about everything she knew about Melissa and her relationship with Kelly Ann and Craig. Melissa's mother revealed that her daughter did have an affair with Craig while living under the same roof as his wife. She also mentioned that Melissa told her about Craig's frequent drug use and that he was slowly becoming more and more violent towards her. Melissa mentioned Kelly Ann too and noted that she was paranoid and unbalanced. The woman would walk around the mansion all night, hallucinating and seeing things that weren't there.

The detectives were now certain that the bodybuilding power couple had something to do with the murder but they still had one loose end, and that was the pickup truck which was seen speeding after the red Jaguar on the night of the murder. The police were still unable to find out who the driver was, or identify the person behind the wheel. They needed to dig deeper and uncover if the killers had any outside help. The first thing they looked at was the telephone records which listed all the calls made on the 13th and 14th December of 2005. One number popped out right away because it was dialed several times that night. The number belonged to Craig's gym friend who would hang out with him during his training sessions. His name was Anthony Gross and he considered Craig Titus his role model. The police officers contacted Gross on December 18th in order to set up an interview because they thought there might be a possible involvement in the crime. Anthony Gross walked into the station the next day with a lawyer by his side. Gross knew that something was up so he wanted to have a head start.

Anthony Gross didn't hold back or try to hide anything. He openly admitted that he was the owner of the pickup truck which was seen on the night of the murder. He told the investigators that Craig Titus called him up sometime before midnight and asked him for a small favor. Craig asked Anthony to meet him at his mansion and help him out with something. Anthony claimed that Craig didn't provide any details over the phone and that he arrived at the house without the prior knowledge that the crime had occurred. The police investigators did confirm that Anthony drove behind the red Jaguar after going through the surveillance footage from a gas station that was located near Kelly Ann's and Craig's house. Anthony got inside and purchased a can of gas. The cars were seen arriving and leaving together.

Anthony told the detectives that they also made a stop at a local Wal-Mart, but Kelly Ann was the one doing the shopping this time. The surveillance confirmed his statements because Kelly Ann was caught on camera sometime around 03:00 AM, buying juice, and a total of seven lighter fluid bottles. The purchase itself was a clear evidence that all three of them were planning to set something on fire. Anthony claimed that his only role that night was help Craig and Kelly Ann get rid of the vehicle. He didn't mention anything about covering up the dead body inside of the trunk. The police had a solid case against the couple so they approached the judge on December 20th who review the collected evidence and issued a warrant for the arrest of Kelly Ann Ryan and Craig Titus. Once they arrived at the mansion, neither of them were home. They were obviously expecting the police, so they fled.

The detectives started questioning Kelly Ann's and Craig's friends because they assumed they might know something about their run from the law. And they were quite right. Both Kelly Ann and Craig were big talkers and they even mentioned to one of their friends that their plan was to go to Boston and hide out until everything blows over. A couple of friends also claimed that Kelly Ann invited them to their mansion on the night of the murder. Craig was there as well and he couldn't stop talking about how disappointed he was in their former assistant who turned out to be a drug addict. However, the things took a strange turn at the end of the night because Craig pretty much confessed to the murder, and even demonstrated how he strangled and beaten Melissa.

According to them, Kelly Ann and Melissa got into an argument and started shouting at each other. They were clearly fighting over Craig and things were getting physical. Craig defended his wife and ended up attacking Melissa. Frequent steroids use is often linked to a phenomenon called roid rage. Since Craig Titus was a well-known steroids user, there is a huge possibility that he snapped that day and simply couldn't control his anger which had a deadly consequence.

Kelly Ann and Craig were on the run for a total of nine days before they got arrested. They stayed in their friends' houses as they traveled across the country in a search of a secure place to hole in. But the tip about their Boston visit turned out to be true because they were arrested right there in that city. Craig Titus was spotted in a parking lot in front of a popular mall while waiting for Kelly Ann. She was in a beauty salon, getting her hair dyed to make her look less recognizable. She took her time and got a manicure as well. They didn't make a huge show out of it and surrendered without any resistance. They were quickly returned to Nevada where a trial was about to start.

The murder trial

During the police interviews which were conducted with both Kelly Ann Ryan and Craig Titus, each of them offered similar accounts on what happened on the night of the murder. Craig was sticking to the story of an accidental overdose and that he needed to get rid of the corpse in order to save his reputation and avoid being prosecuted for a crime he didn't commit. He continued saying that his only goal was to destroy the body and he described what he apparently did in order to make sure Melissa James was never to be found: *"Put a blanket on the ground, grabbed another blanket and I taped up her head. I didn't want to see her face. I didn't want to see her face. I took the tie off one of my robes, and I put it on the back of her neck and pushed her knees up and tied her knees to her chest. Then we wrapped her up in a blanket and taped it up and put her in the trunk. Then I put her in the trunk and dropped her a couple times. Kelly was crying hysterically."*

Kelly Ann Ryan repeated Craig's story. She didn't mention anything about any love triangle, or a fight that probably occurred earlier on the day of the murder. But the police officers had enough testimonies to prove that there was a lot more beneath the surface. Both Kelly Ann Ryan and Craig Titus were facing charges of murder with the use of a deadly weapon, kidnapping, and arson. Anthony Gross did cooperate with the investigators, but he didn't get off so easily. His charges included accessory to murder and arson.

All three of them appeared in front of a judge in the spring of 2008. Their defense lawyers were aware of the strength of the case so they advised their clients to take the plea deal and avoid the jury where they will not stand a chance. The prosecutor had to say this about Kelly Ann and Craig on that day: *"I think both defendants recognize that a train was coming down the tracks and either they resolved it today or we were going to go to a jury trial and leave it up to a jury."* They did make the right decision because the punishment might have been harsher.

Craig pleaded guilty to a murder, arson, and kidnapping. He managed to avoid the death penalty which was on the table if he agreed to go in front of a jury. Titus will stay behind the bars for the next twenty-one to fifty-one years but will be eligible for a parole after serving the majority of his sentence. Since Craig Titus agreed that he was the only one responsible for the murder, Kelly Ann Ryan had been sentenced for the arson, as well as an assault with a deadly weapon, and got six to twenty-six years. She is eligible for a parole now as we speak, and her next hearing is in October of 2017. Kelly Ann Ryan did feel remorse after everything that had happened and here is what she said in front of a judge: *"I am truly, truly sorry. I know I did not kill. But I did aid in the events. I know I was not in a state of mind emotionally or physically to make the right decisions or to, oh God, to take appropriate control of what was happening."*

Anthony Gross did speak to the police early on in the investigation and helped them uncover the crucial evidence that linked the pair to the killing of Melissa James. Gross pleaded guilty to arson and accessory to commit first-degree arson. He was not charged with the murder, probably because he was clever enough to lawyer up as soon as he was summoned to the police headquarters. He was put on probation.

The aftermath

Kelly Ann Ryan is currently locked up in Florence McClure Women's Correctional Center, Nevada. She was granted parole for the assault charges but the board couldn't do the same for arson. Then the appeal was rejected once again in 2014. Now she is hoping that she might be released in the autumn of 2017 because her next parole hearing is just around the corner. Craig Titus is located in Lovelock Correctional Center, Nevada. Kelly Ann is not married to Craig anymore and she filed for a divorce as soon as she received her sentence. The marriage was officially over in winter of 2009.

Murder at the Charisma Ranch

Robert Dorotik was born in 1945, two years before his future wife Jane Marguerite Colvey. It would be 23 years before they would meet and fall in love. They married on April 4, 1970 in Los Angeles California.

Two years later Nicholas was born, another son Alexander would follow shortly after that and by January 16, 1976 their family would be complete with the birth of their daughter Claire Elizabeth.

Robert was an Engineer and Jane was a Health care professional as well as a successful business woman. She made a six figure salary from her 9-5 job alone, and the horse ranch she ran with her daughter was starting to bring in money too.

Robert and Jane would have more than one argument over the money Jane and their daughter Claire spent on Charisma Ranch. He quit his job as an engineer to support Jane's endeavor of raising and training horses. Bob started a business making horse jumps, but by 2000 his business was in trouble. One of the last arguments Jane and Bob had was when Jane and Claire told him they found another horse that would be perfect for the ranch. Robert complained they didn't need any more horses. This infuriated Jane and she told him in no uncertain terms that it was her money and she would spend it how she wanted, she didn't need his permission.

On the afternoon of February 13, 2000 Jane got ready to go down to tend to the horses. Bob was dressing in his jogging clothes and told Jane he was going to go for a run. Bob had been a long distance runner for years. Jane had an injury that prevented her from participating. Jane asked her husband to stoke the fire before he left and she went to the barn.

Mrs. Dorotik returned to the house a couple hours later and Bob was nowhere to be found. She waited a while longer and began looking for him. There were others including neighbors and sons Nick and Alex. Becoming increasingly worried about her husband Jane called the police and told them that he had not come home after his run. A search was organized by the police and in the early morning hours of February 14, 2000 Police found Robert's battered, bloodied body by the side of the road about three miles from home. Police immediately suspected Jane.

Robert Dorotik had died from blunt force trauma and strangulation. He had several injuries to the face and the back of the head (an expert testified the wounds were consistent with a hammer). There were defensive wounds on his hands. He was still wearing his jogging clothes although according to the detectives his shoes were tied in an odd manner. The rope used to strangle him was still around his neck and had made a laceration on his throat.

They did not find blood at the scene that would have been consistent with it being the murder site. Robert had been killed somewhere else and moved here. They found the tire tracks and shoe prints. Jane could not be linked to any of the shoe prints, only the tire tracks. However, hers were not the only tire tracks there, the others were not linked to anyone.

The evidence from the beginning seemed to point at Jane Dorotik as the killer. At the scene where they found the body there were tire tracks that matched the three different treads on her truck. At the residence there was a massive amount of blood that had been cleaned at. Jane claims that the blood was from a nosebleed Robert had and cleaned up. Between the box springs and mattress there was a towel soaked with blood. In a bag in the master bedroom they found a syringe with a horse tranquilizer in it and Jane's fingerprint in Bob's blood was found on it. She was arrested before the blood analysis could even be returned.

Around the room investigators found impact blood spatter patterns as well as drip, transfer and cast off. In one of the closets in the house they found a steam carpet shampooer and a significant amount of cleaning supplies. Bob's blood was found on the cap, handle and nozzle of one of the bottles.

Blood stains consistent with Robert's were found in the bed of the truck Jane, Claire and the ranch hands used around the ranch. They found no blood spatter on his shoes or shirt, but did find some blood on his boxers. One of the two hands never showed up for work the day after Bob's death.

Jane was booked into San Diego County Jail and with the help of family made bail.

Jane's daughter Claire was incriminated in the murder, that she was actually the one that killed Robert, her own father. It was well known that father and daughter had a stormy relationship, and at times became volatile. It was never revealed why the two seemed to hate each other, but Claire even wrote a scathing letter to her father about a "betrayal of trust."

Jane's defense team Kerry Steigerwalt and Cole Casey now had to figure out how to defend their 55 year old client. What they decided on wasn't the most unusual way to do it and it and many other attorneys had done in numerous courtrooms around the country. They deliberately brought Claire up as a suspect. By showing that another person 'could' have committed the murder there is a chance that it will raise enough of a doubt in a jury's mind for them to bring back an acquittal instead of a guilty verdict. This is what the attorney's for Jane were doing, trying to raise a reasonable doubt. This strategy would ultimately tear the family apart. In a letter written three years after her conviction Jane would call her attorney 'ego driven' and the implicating of her daughter a 'seriously flawed defense strategy.'

Prosecutor Bonnie Howard-Regan was convinced that Jane killed her husband to keep from having to pay him spousal support. It seemed there was an impending divorce on the horizon for Bob and Jane. They had separated in 1997 but talked it out and decided to keep their money separate and got back together.

Their own sons commented that their parents' marriage wasn't the most loving and at times their fights became very heated. But is this a motive for murder? Perhaps not just the fights, maybe it was the fact that if the two divorced Jane would have to pay Robert up to 40% of her annual income. This would be upwards of 50,000 dollars a year. Jane was incensed when a divorce attorney had told her that. That is a huge motive for murder in the eyes of the law. There was also a $250,000 life insurance policy on both Bob and Jane. She was forthcoming with the detectives about this during the investigation. If she had to pay that much out in spousal support she wouldn't be able to keep the horse ranch, and it seemed that was all she cared about.

Jane's trial would begin in May of 2001 a little over a year after her husband was murdered. Jane had pled not guilty and was making passionate pleas to the public declaring her innocence. Though her daughter and sister also claimed that Jane was innocent of this heinous crime, Claire, Bonnie Long and a ranch hand all invoked their Fifth Amendment right against self-incrimination. Steigerwalt brought up the fact that Claire's alibi was never confirmed. Had the Sheriff's Department zeroed in on Jane in a hasty attempt to close the case?

On June 9, 2001 the case of Jane Dorotik v The State of California went to the jury for deliberation. After the third day both the defense and the prosecution were starting to worry. Maybe they hadn't presented their case as well as they'd thought. Maybe they didn't explain things in an easy to understand way. In the end however, it wasn't that the jury had a problem understanding what they saw and heard during the trial. They were just being diligent, making sure every juror understood what the evidence was and how it fit in the scheme of things. In fact, they had a unanimous decision on the first vote...guilty on the charge of first degree murder.

Judge Joan Weber said that there was "an overwhelming amount of circumstantial evidence" and when Jane's attorney filed for a new trial it was denied. New witnesses had come forward and Steigerwalt asked that the case be reopened to the jury could hear what they had to say. She denied his request. Weber also asked, "How could you have your husband's blood on your hands if you had nothing to do with his death?" The Judge Weber was referring to the syringe with Janes fingerprint on it. It was an integral piece of evidence in the case.

Without a new trial in San Diego County, the next step is Court Of Appeal Of California, Fourth Appellate District, Division One.

The Court of Appeals works differently than the Trial Court. It is not a place for a new trial or a retrial. They won't look at new evidence or hear from new witnesses. It is strictly for trying to overturn the lower court's decision. If this happens then the Trial Court would be made to do one of several different actions in the case. One would be a whole new trial, which in Jane's case is what her attorney would want to happen. Or perhaps the Appellate Court would order Trial Court to look at additional evidence and/or revisit the facts in the case.

Either of these would be a win for Jane and her defense team. However, before these could happen her attorney would have to show that there was an error in the trial procedure or in how Weber interpreted the law.

This all starts with a Notice to Appeal, and then a brief has to be filed. In many cases appeals are decided based solely on this brief. Other times there will oral arguments before anything is decided.

Janes appeal was filed on November 18, 2003. She is asserting that Judge Weber should have included in the instructions to the jury the lessor charge of voluntary manslaughter because the state didn't present evidence that there was premeditation and aforethought to constitute first degree murder. She was denied.

On June 12, 2009 Jane filed another appeal. There were three key facts in this appeal. In the first one she claims 'ineffective assistance of counsel'. Jane claimed that her defense team didn't represent her properly. They didn't do any investigation of their own.

Second, she believed that not letting the jury hear from the new witnesses and not doing DNA testing jeopardized her case. The rope used to strangle Robert was never test for DNA, claiming that epithelia's of the real killer would have been found.

Third, there were procedural mistakes because of the delayed discovery and her actual innocence.

The defense was not allowed to present evidence that the State's expert witness had many mistakes in other cases by using 'faulty methodology'. The jury was not allowed to hear from an eyewitness.

The Appellate Court denied her, again.

The San Diego Union-Tribune reported on November 22, 2015 that a Judge has determined Jane be allowed to have the DNA in her case tested. The rope used to strangle Bob, the fingernail scrapings, and a piece of hair found around the victim's finger all be tested.

Jane still proclaims her innocence and said the ranch hand that didn't show up for work the day after the murder should be considered. He drives a black pick-up, and his tire tracks were also found at the scene. She also reiterated that the man owed the Dorotik's money.

Jane filed her first appeal on November 18, 2003. The Appellate court upheld the lower court's decision. Then Jane, known also as the petitioner filed Habeas petition on April 4, 2006 in the State Superior Court. Next was a Habeas Petition in the Appellate Court on January 3, 2006. And again Jane filed with the State Supreme Court on November 20, 2006. All appeals and motions to this point had been denied or affirmed the lower court's decision.

On June 1, 2007 Jane would file a Petition for Writ of Habeas Corpus, a Motion to appoint counsel, a Motion for Leave to Proceed in Forma Pauperis and a request for DNA testing. This too was denied or dismissed.

In July of 2007 Jane managed to get the money for filing fees and Magistrate Judge Porter ordered the case be reopened on July 9, 2007.

In the appeal for ineffectual assistance of counsel the superior court "denied the claims on the merits in a written order but only addressed the first two claims. On appeal the Appellate Court did the same thing.

Jane contends that council should have done independent testing of the forensic evidence that the prosecution would be presenting at trial and that there was other available evidence that he could have taken advantage of but didn't. Jane contends that had he done so the findings would have weakened the prosecution's case.

Another point the petitioner brought up is that her counsel didn't call her as a witness in her own defense.

Petitioner wanted a medical professional called as an expert witness to testify as to the medical impossibility that she could have perpetrated the murder due to an injury from an accident years earlier. That she would not have had the strength to do what the prosecution says she did.

Counsel for the defense did not object when a detective testified that he thought she was the killer. He could have also asked for a mistrial also.

He didn't insist on DNA testing prior to the start of the trial, armed with the results of the tests, petitioner is sure that it would have pointed to the real killer or killers.

Petitioner believes that her counsel should have brought up different scenarios that could have explained away the circumstantial evidence brought up at trial.

That he could have provided innocent theories for the incriminating evidence.

He didn't show that police didn't follow any leads, including eyewitnesses that came forward in the early stages of the investigation; they made up their mind that she was guilty. Therefore they didn't look for the real killer/killers.

Jane contends that her counsel could have done their own investigation and found the witnesses that were not heard at trial. Instead he made the leap to blaming Claire Dorotik as a defense.

And finally, follow through on the promises counsel made to the jury about what the evidence would show, and not make a comment to the affect that Jane was guilty.

If none of these ten points were true but the last one, would that fact that her own defense counsel made a comment that directly or indirectly told the jury he thought she was guilty should have been grounds for a mistrial and perhaps proceedings started to disbar her attorney.

The points brought up in Jane's eyes caused her to be wrongly convicted for the murder of her husband.

The forensic evidence in many parts does not support the prosecution's theory. Think about the "blood" found on the wall that supposedly dripped down from the master bedroom upstairs. The man who sold /rented the property to the Dorotik's knew of a water leak. Rain water would get in the track of the sliding door and seep down the wall of the stairs leading to the bedroom. There was Bob's DNA there, but was it from blood? Walking shirtless up the stairs and rubbing his sweaty arm on the wall could leave his DNA, it was not said that it was blood.

Post-conviction reports showed that there was way less blood present than would have been if the State's expert witness, Merrit, were correct. McDonell who did the post-conviction report says the fatal blow probably occurred outside the bedroom. But at the same time doesn't accept the idea that Bob was killed where he was found or that he was killed somewhere else, body dumped where it was found and the blood evidence planted.

McDonell also said that the blood on the mattress could have easily been caused by a bloody nose. That being said it still doesn't explain the different blood stain patterns found throughout the room.

Those where found on the pillow, nightstand, walls, bedspread and the window. Those he said cannot be explained away by a nosebleed.

The post-conviction report says that Merrit's testimony was wrong inasmuch as there was not enough blood soaked in to support his idea that Bob remained on the mattress for a long time after the attack.

McDonell concurs with petitioner that the blood around the pot-belly stove could very well have been from the nosebleed. Petitioner wants further testing to find out if it even had anything to do with the murder at all.

The bloody thumb print on the syringe was due to Bob helping Jane with a vet procedure. There was a horse tranquilizer inside the syringe and Jane's thumbprint in Bob's blood on it. This was admitted into evidence? Why, it's said to be a 'key piece' of evidence in the prosecution's case. Petitioner's counsel didn't object? Per Bob's toxicology report there was no drugs in his system. How did they tie it into the murder?

The truck, tire tracks and shoe prints. There was much to do about the tire tracks at the scene where Bob's body was found. There were actually two sets, one belonging to the family truck, the one that everyone including the farm hands had access to. But there was another set, never identified. The shoe prints found also at the scene couldn't be attributed to Jane either. Both sets were too big. The tracks that showed Jane's truck had backed up at the spot where the body was found can easily be explained as well. Bob used the truck to measure jogging routes. If he were to come to the exact length he wanted, he would have just turned around at that spot, hence the backup tracks.

A cursory search of the house was done the evening that Jane reported Bob missing. Police and Police dogs were all in the house including the master bedroom. They didn't find any blood.

Jane was in an accident in 1983 and had a severe injury to a hip which had to be put back together with metal and screws. The prosecution says that Jane would have bludgeoned her husband, then carried him down the stairs from the bedroom, through the house, across a 60' porch and lifted him into the back of a full sized Ford F250. Defense counsel should have brought up the fact that his client couldn't have done any of that. The Appellate court says that her sons saw her pulling irrigation pipes around the ranch that weighed about 75 lbs. pulling on 75lbs of something is different than lifting 147 lbs of dead weight.

Detective Richard Empson when questioned about the rope used to strangle Robert Dorotik and why it wasn't tested for DNA said the "criminologists in his office discouraged testing it because too many people had handled it." When pressed about the possibility of DNA on it that could have belonged to Claire or the ranch hand Leonel Morales or someone else and lead to the real killer, what then? Empson continued, "I believe I know who killed Bob Dorotik, that's why I arrested Jane Dorotik." Personal opinions are not supposed to be brought in to testimony, especially from an officer of the court. Did Jane's counsel object to this? Did it prejudice the jury against the petitioner? It could be said that it inflamed the jury. Most jurors will believe a law enforcement officer over anyone else. Even if the comment was objected to and stricken from the record the juror's still heard it and no matter if they are told to disregard it, it will still be in their mind.

There are so many points that Jane brought up on each one of her appeals. And each and every one of them were dismissed by the Courts. Many of Jane's friends and family still believe that Jane is innocent and should at least get a new trial so all of the evidence can be heard and that maybe she can even testify in her own defense. Although her trial court attorney believed that doing so was not a good idea. Clearly he didn't believe his client was innocent of the crime.

In the findings of the Appellate Court they say that the petitioner didn't show how not having the jury hear that Merrit's methodology was flawed and that he had been wrong on other cases would not have changed the jury's verdict.

They stated that even though the petitioner believes that the prosecution purposefully did not test for DNA she cannot prove how it would have changed anything. Also added the testing would not have brought forth any exculpatory or impeaching evidence. Knowing that DNA has set wrongfully convicted people free by proving their innocence this statement seems wrong in its entirety. Jane would be in a Catch 22 scenario, she can't prove that by not testing there was an error in law and without being able to prove it would help her case they wouldn't allow the testing.

Jane says she's been through a living hell since being sent to Chowchilla's prison facility in central California. But she hasn't been wasting her time. Along with filing the above mentioned appeals she is fighting for her fellow prisoners who are over the age of 55.

Jane is appalled at how many women are incarcerated and how the number keeps growing every year. She was once a mental health professional and says that a large number of women in prison should be in a Mental Health facility.

According to Jane "Medical care is liken to a third world country." And "there are women dying in prison alone and unnoticed by prison staff.

What she is trying to get done is this, have more compassionate releases, the parole board has the authority to do this but won't. So a program is working its way through legislation in the state of California. "If The Risk Is Low, Let Them Go".

Jane isn't advocating opening the flood gates and letting these women head off to parts unknown. There are a certain set of criteria in place to make sure the risk is actually low.

First of all, they have to have served at least 50% of their sentence or seven years.

They can't have had any disciplinary actions in the past five years. In other words they have to be a model prisoner.

They cannot have any other felony convictions of their record and they must have a concrete, safe place to stay in the community

These are safeguards to keep reoffenders inside the prison walls. Jane is very passionate about this program. She has watched many of what she calls "Golden Girls" languishing with terminal illnesses for years, alone, not able to be with family because Chowchilla houses inmates from all over the state.

Many of the families just don't have the money or time to be able to travel to see their loved ones. And even the children have to be patted down before they can go in to see a relative, to possibly say a last goodbye.

Jane's alternative custody program has to clear through law makers and with the help of different advocates it's headed in the right direction thanks to Carol Lui a senator from California.

This is being heralded as a great program to help with overcrowding of the prisons in California, and if this comes about in a timely manner it could help Jane as well. She is now 68 years old.

GIRL STRANGLER :
THE TRUE STORY OF SERIAL KILLER

DANA SUE GRAY

27

ERIN PIERC

Dana Sue Gray was born on December 6th, 1957 in Pasadena, California. Her mother, Beverly Arnett, was a former beauty queen who worked as a professional model. Her father, Russell Armbrust, worked as a hairdresser and was married three times prior to marrying Beverly. The couple had several miscarriages before Dana was born.

Her mother was born for the camera and loved attention. She liked being pampered, getting her make-up done and wearing flashy outfits. Beverly modeled for Bullock's, did print ads for Hamilton watches and was once a Rose Princess at the Tournament of Roses Parade.

LIKE MOTHER LIKE DAUGHTER

Russell divorced Beverly, however, when he witnessed his wife attack an older woman that had angered her. Beverly had also maxed out his credit cards, putting him financial peril. Dana was only two years old at the time of the divorce and rarely saw her father.

"Some kind of estrangement had taken place," forensic psychologist Lora Dixon said. "After her parents divorced she had turned down invitations in her teen years to visit her father on all of the holidays and birthday get-togethers."

"There is also something to think about here in terms of Beverly's own temper. Dana clearly witnessed violence and bullying from her mother at an early age. She inherited those characteristics from her mother with tragic results."

Dana had discipline problems early on as she sought attention from her narcissistic mother. Her mother would discipline her but Dana would retaliate by stealing money to buy candy. Her mother had two other children from a previous marriage. Dana would go into the rooms of her step brothers and urinate in their beds.

Her mother would continue to try and discipline her to no avail as Dana would lash back with violence. This facet of her personality was never placed under her control.

"Mommy and daughter didn't get along," Dixon said. "But obviously that isn't unusual nor does mean she was destined to become a serial killer. There was some deep seated issues festering here though. This is evident when Dana gave her mother a snake for Christmas. 'A snake for a snake' the card must have read."

Nonetheless, it did not appear on the surface that Dana had to endure the brutal childhood that gave birth to so many other serial killers. Cedric Ward, one of her step brothers, did admit that Dana did not have the best of childhoods. "It was not happy growing up," he recalled.

SCHOOL AND SEX

Dana did not get along with other students and achieved low grades in all of her classes. She was a chronic truancy case and often forged notes to get out of class. Dara was sexually active at a very early age as she would lose her virginity at the age of twelve. She would ultimately go from one relationship to the next, using sex to lure men into her web of narcissism.

"Dana has a problem," said Richard Singer, a boyfriend of her mother. "She does not want to be told no. She has her own thing, and nobody could tell her any different. You could not tell Dana what to do."

"Her mother would pretty much try to control her, but Dana would go off on you. You could not tell her what to do. Dana is very hyperactive and opinionated."

During her adolescent years, she loved horror movies and read Grimm's Fairy Tales numerous times. As a teenager, she and a neighbor built a catapult. They would tie tiny parachutes on the cat's backs and then hurl them into the air, with the parachute carrying them down into neighborhood swimming pools.

A MOTHER'S DEATH

Beverly contracted breast cancer when Dana was fourteen. Dana decided to become a nurse after witnessing the way the nurses at the hospital treated her mother. Her mother died and Dana was forced back to live with her father.

"The temptation here is to say that Dana was inspired to become a nurse by witnessing the compassion the nurses shown her mother during her illness," Dixon said. "But I would posit a different psychological scenario. Dana saw that the nurses had power over her mother. That for once, her mother was weak and had to defer to other people for the first time in her life. Dana wanted power. Control. What better way to get that then to become a nurse?"

Dana went into a depression after her mother died and would reveal her sentimentality in letters she would write to her then boyfriend, Don Lane, in jail.

"Tomorrow, Good Friday, 4-1-94, is also April Fool's and also my real mom's 76th B-day. It's been 22 years since her death, and I still celebrate her B-day for her. I celebrate it for her 'cause she died when I was 14 and we never got to get past the 'grow years' to become friends like my dad and I are. She was wild-but made my younger years a total adventure: camping, clamming @ Pismo, best Halloween parties and the best Xmases a poor family could have. She could make a fun time out of just anything."

"Again, you see in her letters a sense of victimhood," Dixon said. "She makes no mention of her mother ignoring her birthdays. And she describes her family as 'poor.' They lived in relatively affluent area, becoming strapped for cash primarily because of Beverly's spending."

GROWING UP

Dana's father Russell had remarried, living with his new wife Yvonne who had a daughter named Cathy. Dana would move in with the couple, sharing a room with Cathy. The reunion between her and her father would be a short-lived one, however, as Yvonne would find marijuana in Dana's room.

Russell's wife then kicked Dana out of the home.

On her own at the age of fifteen, Dana would move-in with her sky-diving instructor, Rob Beaudry. The union would produce two pregnancies but Rob talked Dana in to getting abortions both times. These were decisions that she would later come to resent.

At five-foot-two and weighing a stocky 135 lbs, Dana would nonetheless inherit her mother's penchant for fancy clothes and desire to be pampered with manicures and pedicures. Despite her taste in high-end living, associates would describe her appearance and demeanor as "hard."

She would graduate from Newport High School in 1976 and enter nursing school at Saddleback College in Mission Viejo, California. Dana paid her way through nursing school while working as waitress. She also taught herself screen printing techniques and sold screen printed items for extra cash.

"Dana inherited her mother's psychology when it came to money and relationships," Dixon said. "She operated from a 'lack mindset', in that she always saw herself as poor. She was industrious but felt sorry for herself that she had to work so hard, paying her way through school and working for a living. The shopping sprees were a relief to her perceived burden."

ESTRANGED FROM FAMILY

Dana became estranged from her half-brothers, her older siblings from Beverly's previous marriage. The reasons were always financial as she become embroiled in a dispute over the proceedings from their aunt's estate.

She had run-ins with her half-brother Rick in particular.

Dana reacted with anger after he told her to sell belongings to pay her mounting bills. Rick wrote back telling her that she had no consideration for others.

"Nuts," is how her sister-in-law described her. "Not even normally greedy. Crazy. Gray is missing a conscience. I do not think it is there. When you talk to her, she has no concept of other human beings."

"The half-brothers clearly knew she was trouble," Dixon said. "They did the right thing in distancing themselves.

NURSING CAREER.

Immediately upon graduating from Saddleback, Dana landed a nursing job at Corona Community Hospital. She used that as a springboard to a high paying position as an operating room nurse at Inland Valley Regional Medical Center (some reports have her identified as a labor and delivery nurse). She was described by one nursing supervisor as "very caring."

During this time, she had found another boyfriend, a windsurfer whom she would accompany on trips to Hawaii where they would pursue various outdoor activities. This relationship would be an on-again, off-again type deal until Dana would marry Tom Gray. The couple would tie the knot at a winery in the affluent Temecula area.

Tom was an active sportsman and had a crush on Dana since high school.

"She was a hard core athlete," Tom recalled. "A sky diver, wind surfer, mountain bike enthusiast and snorkeler, and she was skilled in each sport."

Dana took pride in her physical strength and would often roll up her sleeve to reveal her bicep muscle. 'She how strong I am?' she would ask.

Living in the gated community of the affluent Canyon Lake suited Dana as it would have been something that would have pleased her mother. Her and Tom started numerous businesses where they used the name "Graymatter."

Tom could not stop Dana's spending habits, however. The couple took out a loan for $47,000 and another for $20,000 within the first nine months of their marriage.

"She was replicating the marriage of her mother and father," Dixon said. "She liked the empowerment that came from having a lot of money. Having money, or rather the act of spending money is what fed her ego. Only in Dana's case she took it way beyond her mother. She was willing to kill for that feeling."

The marriage quickly soured when Dana's spending habits sent the couple into overwhelming consumer debt. Her alcoholism also worsened, particularly after she suffered a miscarriage. Dana indulged in three or four glasses of wine while cooking dinner and then having more with the dinner itself. Her days off from the hospital were adventures in bourbon whiskey, 7-Up and Tequila shooters. Later, she would admit to using marijuana and cocaine.

When Gray unexpectedly received a $7500 inheritance, Dana took the money and blew it on a trip to Europe, leaving her husband behind at home. When she returned , she began an affair with Don Lane, a musician in her husband's band. When Lane agreed to support her, she moved out of the Canyon Lake house and spent $11,000 in five months.

In March of 1992, however, Dana began seeing a psychiatrist. He prescribed Paxil for her, probably to stave off depression among other things.

Lane had a five year old son at the time and would later tell authorities of Dana's "mood changes" and her propensity to break out into "hysterical tears" with little provocation.

She filed for divorce from Tom but this would not be finalized until much later. In September of 1993, Tom and Dana were forced to file for bankruptcy to prevent foreclosure on their Canyon Lake residence.

Despite the value of the home increasing, the amount they owed on the house was more than its worth. They owed $177,500 on a house valued at $125,000 because of double mortgages.

She suffered a miscarriage, exacerbating more depression as well as alcohol and drug abuse.

FIRED FROM THE HOSPITAL

The trouble continued for Dana as two months later she would be fired from the hospital for stealing Demerol and other opiate pain killers.

"What Dana was trying to do was medicate herself," Dixon said. "The new marriage, the exotic vacations, the fancy house and cars. It was never enough to quell the demons that spoke in her head. A control freak out of control. So she struggled to constantly fill the void with booze and drugs. Then this spirals into an affair with a friend of her husband. Again, this life trajectory happens to a lot of people. In Dana's case, however, she needed that extra thrill. Something more than the rush of sky-diving, cheating on her husband, and getting high. She needed the ultimate adrenaline rush. The power to take someone's life."

TIME TO KILL

In later reports, hospital authorities would reveal their own problems with Gray.

"She is sarcastic," Darlena Addison, the former nursing supervisor who fired Gray for stealing drugs. "She does get her point across if she's crossed or doesn't get her way."

"The problem was a condescending attitude, as Dana believed that she was smarter than everyone and had a need to dominate."

The hospital would later report that they did not have any "unusual" deaths during Gray's tenure.

"Of course that is what you would expect them to say," Dixon said. "If they admit to any 'unusual' deaths then it certainly opens them up to a lawsuit. The opportunity would certainly be there for Dana to steal credit cards from elderly patients and rack up bills. It appears, however, that she did not put her murderous impulses into action until after her dismissal. Dana fell in love with the struggle. The fight of her victim as long as she would emerge on he winning end. Poisoning her victims to death in the way it would have been possible for her as a nurse would not have given her that adrenaline rush."

After the loss of her job, Dana would amp up her indulgences in alcohol, drinking straight Vodka, loving the Smirnoff brand in particular.

On Valentine's Day in 1994, Dana contacted Tom's parents (after their separation he had kept his phone number and address a secret). She informed Tom's parents that she wanted to meet with him.

Tom agreed at first but later did not show up.

Tom would find out that Dana had taken out an insurance policy on him without his knowledge. The policy payout would have been enough to pay down the Canyon Lake home the couple used to share.

Later that day, Dana murdered Norma Davis.

THE FIRST VICTIM

Norma Davis was 86 years old at the time. She was the mother-in-law of the woman (Jeri Davis Armbrust) who married Dana's father in 1988. Jeri's first husband, Bill Davis, was Norma's son. Bill died in the early 1980s, and his widow married a newly divorced Russell.

But Jeri continued to care for her elderly mother-in-law, even after she remarried. Dana would also come to know Norma very well.

On February 16th, 1994, however, the body of Norma Davis would be found by a neighbor named Alice Williams. She had been dead for two days as someone had stabbed her in the neck with a wood-handled utility knife. The blade had been inserted so deep that it nearly severed Norma's head.

She also had a filet knife sticking out of her chest.

Police would discover no forced entry into the home. Norma always kept the doors locked unless she was expecting a visitor. Her neighbor, Alice, stated that she could not remember if Norma had mentioned she was expecting company.

"We didn't have a lot of information," Detective Joe Greco said. "The only piece of evidence that we had was the entry way of the condominium. There was a faint shoe print on the condominium and it was a 6 ½ size shoe."

Detectives would find the Nike shoe print and Davis' Social Security check in plain view. Additionally, on the first floor of the condo, they found a smear of blood on an armchair and a torn phone cord.

A modus operandi had been established. Dana would manually strangle her victims with a phone cord, then use an object to smash or stab.

The coroner concluded that Norma Davis was strangled first then stabbed. She was stabbed eleven times with Dana leaving the knives stuck in her body.

Police described the scene as one of the most brutal they had ever encountered.

"It was a shock because it was only my second homicide case as a detective," Greco said. "It was overwhelming. It crossed my mind that I had a serial killer on my hands."

SHE DEVIL ON A RAMPAGE

"The community was very affluent," Greco said. "They don't have a lot of homicides."

On February 28th, 1994, 66-year old June Roberts was found murdered. She had lived in the gated community of Canyon Lake along with Dana.

Dana had known Roberts and visited her that day saying that she wanted to borrow a book about either overcoming alcohol addiction or vitamins, the reports vary. Dana had her boyfriend's five year old son waiting out in front in her Cadillac.

Ignorant of Dana's true motives, Roberts allowed Dana into her home. She went to retrieve the book Dana inquired about while her would-be killer ripped out the cords to June's phone

Dana would later describe their interaction taking a turn when she became "really annoyed" that June came back with the wrong book. She also told a psychologist that she became infuriated that June allegedly said that she "didn't do enough" to save her marriage with Tom.

When asked what made Dana believe that Roberts and her other victims were looking down on her, Dana responded that she did not like their body language.

"The arching of the eyebrow," Dana said. "That is what happened. All three."

Dana then used the phone cord to strangle Roberts to death.

"I was right behind her," Dana recalled. "I choked her with the phone cord. She was holding on, trying to get the cord off. I pulled her down. She was on her back. I hit her in the head with a bottle. I lost it. I was so consumed. I don't know the time span in there-must have been very quick. She must have stopped moving, and I left. As I walked out, she had a little wallet thing. I grabbed it."

"We went out and proceeded to shop up a storm. "

In talking to psychologists,.Dana appeared unaware of the concept of remorse.

"It was very brutal," Greco said. "The victim had been strangled with her own telephone cord and actually tied to a chair. And she was struck so hard (by the wine bottle) she fractured her skull."

Her autopsy noted a "moderately deep ligature furrow" and a "6 x 3 purple contusion." The cranium contusion was caused by a heavy glass wine bottle striking her with tremendous force. The volume of blood in and near the bathroom door, the walls and pooling under the body made it impossible to gauge the age of the victim.

"This is when the profile of Dana Sue becomes highly unusual," Dixon said. "With female serial killers, you usually see poison or the use of a gun as the weapon of choice. Dana Sue, however, approached her victims with a high level of physical violence that rivaled a male serial killer. There was nothing lady-like about her approach. She was a cold blooded, hands on killer."

TIME TO SHOP

Dana did not hesitate after murdering Roberts, she had to get her shopping fix met.

She would go to Bally's Wine Country Cafe in Temecula, eat crab cake and scampi while charging the meal to Robert's credit card. She could not finish the entire meal, however, and had the waitress pack the rest.

She then got an eyebrow wax and a perm then treated her boyfriend's son to a stylish haircut.

"The fact that she had the little boy accompany her on both the murders and the shopping trips deserves mention," Dixon said. "Dana remained childless throughout life. She was regretted getting two abortions and suffered a miscarriage during her marriage with Tom. Going out and about with her boyfriend's son made her feel like a Mommy. She could be the Mommy that she never had, treating the young child to things she always wanted."

Dana signed "June Roberts" on the $164.76 charge at the salon. She then went to the mall and spent $511 on a black suede jacket, several pairs of cowboy boots, and then $161 on a pair of diamond earrings all charged to Roberts. Her addiction still not satiated, she went to a drug store, picking up dog treats, two bottles of Smirnoff and a toy police helicopter for the boy.

The day after, Dana loaded up on suntan lotion, got a massage at Murrieta Hot Springs resort and then went on another power shopping spree.

"She had absolutely no remorse," Dixon said. "There was no hiding out and laying low like some other wimpy male serial killer. Dana Sue was different. She killed and then she had to do the one thing that gratified her. She had to get to the mall. She had to get the high from buying stuff. She had to enjoy the power while it still lasted."

Ironically, none of her victims had anything stolen aside from their credit cards.

"Dana didn't take any rings from her victims," Greco said. "Or some valuables from the home that were obvious. So I don't think any of the crimes were motivated by money."

Ten days after the Roberts' murder, Dana would enter an antique store, the Main Street Trading Post in Lake Elsinore. Dana stated to the cashier, Dorinda Hawkins, that she wanted to buy a picture frame for a photo of her deceased mother.

"Dana came in asking about picture frames," Greco said. "During their interaction, Dana felt that Dorinda was being condescending to her.

"I felt sick to my stomach," Dana said. "I wanted to vomit. I wanted her to die."

Dana asked if Hawkins was working alone and then she attacked her, strangling her with the store's telephone cord.

"Dorinda is begging for her life when Dana is strangling her," Greco said. "And Dorinda told her 'you can have anything you want. Take the cash, I have eight kids, just let me live.' And Dana told her 'I'm not doing this for the money.' She said that twice. And that really gives you an insight on what Dana is thinking while she's committing these crimes."

Dorinda, however, continued to fight, resisting Dana all the way.

"Relax," Dana said, trying to coax Hawkins into dying. "Just relax."

Hawkins grabbed a broom and poked Dana with it to no avail.

Dana then shoved Hawkins to the ground and stepped on her head as a brace to better choke her.

"Her eyes were flat," Hawkins recalled. "I could tell she had killed before."

Believing her victim dead, Dana stole five dollars from Hawkins' purse and twenty dollars from the cash register.

An hour later, she began another shopping spree, still using Roberts' credit cards.

Hawkins, however, would survive the attack and provide the police the required description of Dana.

THE ATTACKS CONTINUE

Nearly a month after her first killing, on March 16th, 1994, Dana would kill the 87-year old Dora Beebe.

Moments after Beebe arrived home from a doctor's appointment, Dana pulled up in front of her house. She knocked on the door and asked Beebe for directions.

"Here we see Dana getting bolder," Dixon said. "With Norma Davis and June Roberts, she knew the victims beforehand. And the attempted murder in the antique store seemed to be a spur of the moment thing. But the Beebe murder is the first occasion where Dana has picked out a stranger. Elderly women were her preferred target, specifically those who were alone, and tragically Beebe emerged in her cross-hairs."

Living in the same neighborhood for several years, it was improbable for Dana to become lost. But she used that as an excuse when she came knocking on Beebe's door asking for directions.

Dana became angry when Beebe said "I don't have time for this." She was able to hide her anger as Beebe capitulated and allowed Dana insider her home to look at a map. Once inside the home, however, Dana assaulted the elderly woman.

'She turned her back on me," Dana said. "I choked her with the phone cord. I hit her in the head with an iron. As I remember it, it wasn't much of a fight."

Using a stainless steel Black and Decker iron that Dana found in the home, Dana bashed Beebe in the head so hard that it dented the appliance.

Less then an hour later, Dana would be at the mall with Beebe's credit cards in hand.

"She enjoyed doing things that were risky," Greco said. "She was a thrill seeker. I think that she really enjoyed what she was doing. She got a thrill out of it."

PANIC IN THE STREETS

The residents in the gated community of Canyon Lake went into panic mode. Some of the elderly citizens moved in with family until the killer was caught. A group of elderly widows organized themselves to sleep together at designated houses, not wanting to be alone.

There were some who thought the killings where the product of a cult engaging in the ritual sacrifice of the elderly.

"Rumors circulated around the entire community," Dixon said. "A terrifying time for everyone, the elderly in particular. This was a relatively well-to-do neighborhood. People were unused to killings, let alone a serial killer. Numerous people bought guns and kept it by their bedside while others banded together in the belief that there were safety in numbers."

FALSE SUSPECT

Police detectives were at a loss early on in finding a suspect. Prospects were so bleak that a supervisor in charge had seriously thought about using a psychic. Dana was not anywhere near the police's list of possible killers. Instead, the police initially suspected that her mother-in-law, Jeri Armbrust, might be the killer.

The police determined that Armbrust used to be married to Davis' son and continued to care for her former mother-in-law.

Detectives grew suspicious because it was unusual that Jeri would continue to take care of someone who was not a blood relative. Norma Davis herself was on death's door, recovering from a triple bypass surgery.

Police determined that Jeri had been in Davis' house the Sunday before the murder and that she wore a pair of Nike shoes.

Jeri stated that she did come to Davis' house but only came to drop off groceries. She heard the TV on upstairs but did not go up to say hello. She left the groceries on the counter and went home.

Police questioned why she didn't say hello but after weeks of questioning police determined that Jeri was not a suspect. She instead became an ally to the investigation.

CAPTURE

Descriptions obtained from the various merchants at the shopping center were eventually used to catch Dana. She had been buying so much stuff that the credit card company called June Roberts' family to inquire about the excessive spending.

Police detectives went to all of the stores where Roberts' credit card had been used, interviewing the cashiers. They obtained a physical description of Dana, surmising that the killer had dyed her hair recently and was accompanied by a little boy.

Detective Greco relayed this information to Jeri Armbrust.

Jeri surmised that the killer was in fact, her step-daughter Dana. She said that Dana recently dyed her hair red and had a boyfriend who had a young son.

Greco then obtained a search warrant and called for the aid of ARCNET (Allied Riverside County Narcotics Enforcement Team) to stake out Gray's home in Lake Elsinore.

Unfortunately, Dana was murdering Dora Beebe just hours before they determined her to be the killer. They followed Dana to a bank where she used Beebe's credit card and then went out for another shopping spree.

"We were able to follow the paper trail created by the use of these credit cards," Greco said. "With the merchants we were able to get a general description of the suspect."

Later that day, Greco arrested Dana while she was cooking dinner. Assisting officers took her boyfriend and his son in for questioning.

HOUSE OF STOLEN GOODS

Police did a thorough search of Dana's home after her arrest.

"They found jewelry, food, liquor, a ski mask, a purse with nearly $2,000 stuck in the washing machine, and many items of clothing," one report stated. "The police obtained a wealth of evidence: Gray's use of credit cards, clerks who had seen her directly after each murder, handwriting experts who identified her signatures on various items."

Dana was interrogated for hours.

"In the interview," Greco recalled. "Dana talked about finding a purse. And that purse belonged to a woman by the name of Dora Beebe. I knew that I had the right suspect in this case. But I didn't not know that on the same day we were serving her search warrant she was killing her last victim."

Dana stated that she never took the credit cards but after police revealed that they had evidence of her using them, Dana claimed that she found both Roberts' and Beebe's cards.

She maintained this story throughout the questioning. When asked why she kept the cards she said that she "had an overwhelming need to shop."

NO REMORSE, NO SYMPATHY

Dana displayed no sympathy for the victims. One psychologist noted that some of Dana's answers were like a robot answering in a manner they believed a normal human should.

After a hearing, Deputy District Attorney Richard Bentley wanted the death penalty. Dana pleaded insanity for all charges. But a witness came forward and stated that she saw Dana at Roberts' house on the day of her death, Dana quickly changed her plea to guilty and robbing and murdering two women as well as the attempted murder at the antique shop.

"At the end of the day," Dixon said. "Dana didn't want to die. When a witness came forward and said she saw Dana at the Roberts' house perhaps she knew that she was done for and would have been executed. Maybe she did not have enough confidence in her ability to pull off the insanity defense. So she struck a deal. She would plead guilty and avoid the death penalty."

Nonetheless, prosecutors were still unable to determine how Dana left the bloody crime scenes without a speck of blood on her or any sign of a struggle. All the clerks and waitresses spotted nothing out of the usual.

LIFE WITHOUT PAROLE

On October 16th, 1998, Dana Sue Gray was sentenced to life without parole.

"It's hard to find words to describe the atrocity in this case," Judge Patrick Magers said during Dana's sentencing. "The crimes were horrendous, callous and despicable."

Dana is currently jailed at the California Women's Prison in Chowchilla.

"She enjoyed the power," Dixon said. "She got addicted to the power she obtained while she killed people who were helpless to fight back. She liked watching them struggle. Liked having control over them before they died."

Jail has not seemed to bother Dana as she referred to her incarceration as her "county condo." She continues to pester her jailers to replicate her high-maintenance civilian lifestyle. She insists on a vegetarian diet and wants the use of a chiropractor. She has requested a mirror and has lobbied consistently for the return of her belongings.

Dana has drawn chilling clown faces, cobbling her paints together from M&M's candy coating, cherry drink mix, lipstick and and baby powder.

Her family came to visit her and brought her a pair of cheap Nike's. She refused them, wanting the high-end models.

Dana continues to thumb her nose at authorities as she sometimes sends collectibles to "murderablia" websites. She has sold her panties at $250, where she autographs them and writes in her prison identification number. She sells her hand tracing for $65 and a 'prison worn shirt', decorated with a drawing of a blue butterfly perched on a skeleton's hand.

"We can look back and say that she was simply psychotic," Dixon said. "And it is really easy to dismiss her killings as someone who was simply crazy violent and not read into it anymore than that. But in looking at the ages and gender of the victim, we can see the connection. All of her victims were old enough to be her mother. So perhaps in Dana's mind she saw her victims as substitutes for her late mother with whom had a lot of anger toward. And I mean violent, aggressive anger. So when she subdued her victims with the phone cord, she would unleash a torrent of rage, smashing them with irons, stabbing them with utility knives,bashing them over the head with wine bottles. She would attack them and have flashbacks of her battles with her Mom, doing things to the victim that she was powerless to do to her mother as a little girl."

"She was doing it all for Mommy."

THE HILLSIDE STRANGLERS

48

NAOMI ROBERTS

Cousins Kenneth Bianchi and Angelo Buono, Jr. are collectively known by their media epithet "The Hillside Strangler". These two men were responsible for the murders of at least nine females, ages 12 to 28, during the late 1970s in Los Angeles, California, and Bianchi killed two more in Washington. After their first three victims did not gain much attention because they were prostitutes, Bianchi and Buono decided to abduct and murder middle-class "nice" girls. Five victims were found on hillsides in the Glendale-Highland Park area during Thanksgiving weekend in 1977 and the resulting panic led to the coining of the moniker "Hillside Strangler".

Lead Los Angeles Police Department homicide investigator Detective Sergeant Bob Grogan, along with his partner Dudley Varney as well as Los Angeles Sheriff's Department's Detective Frank Salerno, believed that the murders were the work of more than one killer but figured the less the murderers knew about what police knew the better.

Bianchi later moved to Washington where he murdered two more women before being caught.

Both Bianchi and Buono were convicted of multiple counts of first-degree murder and sentenced to life. Buono dies of a heart attack on 21 September 2002 while serving his time in Calipatria State Prison in Calipatria, California. Bianchi continues to serve his sentence at Washington State Penitentiary in Walla Walla.

Early Lives

Kenneth Bianchi

Kenneth Alessio Bianchi was born on 22 May 1951 in Rochester, New York, to a 17-year-old alcoholic prostitute who gave him up for adoption two weeks after he was born. He was adopted by Nicholas Bianchi and Frances Sciolono and despite a stable upbringing, Bianchi became a pathological liar at a very early age. Further, as a result of petit mal seizures he suffered at the age of five, Bianchi often daydreamt as if he were in a trance.

Bianchi suffered from insomnia and frequently wet the bed as a child (one of the triad symptoms of serial killers). Frances took him to the doctor on multiple occasions for his urination problem and being examined by the doctor caused Bianchi much embarrassment and humiliation. He also had a bad temper and was diagnosed with passive-aggressive personality disorder which is characterized by an individual who may appear to be enthusiastic about and actively comply with others' desires and needs while simultaneously resisting them, thus resulting in increased anger and hostility. At the core of this disorder is that the sufferer resents responsibility and instead of openly expressing his or her feelings, demonstrates said resentment through actions such as procrastination, forgetfulness, and inefficiency. Despite having a rather high IQ of 116, Bianchi was a chronic underachiever in school. When Frances took him to a psychologist, it was determined that Bianchi was overly dependent upon his mother.

On 2 January 1957, Bianchi fell off of a jungle gym and landed on his face. His mother then sent him to a private Catholic elementary school where he excelled in creative writing. In July 1963, Bianchi pulled down a six-year-old girl's pants after "spontaneously decid[ing] that he liked doing so".

His adoptive father died in 1964, thus leaving an unemotional Bianchi having to attend public high school where he joined a motorcycle club and dated frequently. His adoptive mother was forced to work and she was known for keeping Bianchi home from school for extended periods of time.

While in high school, Bianchi set high standards for his many girlfriends such as complete fidelity and outwardly absolute devotion; however, these standard did not apply to him.

He graduated in 1971 from Gates-Chili High School in Rochester and, soon after, married his high school sweetheart, Brenda Beck; however, the couple divorced after only eight months. Rumor has it that Brenda left without a word.

Bianchi enrolled at Monroe Community College to study police science and psychology after deciding that he wanted to become a police officer; however, after only one term he dropped out and then was rejected for several positions both in Rochester and, later, Los Angeles. Consequently, Bianchi worked a series of menial odd jobs, eventually becoming a jewelry store security guard for which he was fired for stealing and giving his girlfriends the stolen jewelry. He would steal from other employers over the years.

He then left Rochester and moved to Los Angeles in late 1975 at the age of 26.

Angelo Buono, Jr.

Angelo Anthony Buono, Jr. was born on 5 October 1934, also in Rochester, New York, to first-generation Italian-American immigrants originally from San Buono, Italy. His parents divorced when he was young and a five-year-old Buono moved to Glendale, California, with his mother Jenny and his sister Cecilia, where his mother supported the family by doing piecework in a shoe factory. Raised Catholic, this had no effect on Buono's development as a decent human being.

Buono displayed a very high interest in sex from a young age and when he was a teenager claimed that he had raped and sodomized number of girls. Buono idealized serial rapist Caryl Chessman, also known as "The Red Light Bandit", calling Chessman his hero but added that Chessman should have murdered his victims. He developed a deep loathing of women and desire to injure and humiliate them, including his mother who he would verbally abuse; however, he was emotionally tied to her until her death in 1978.

Buono began stealing cars and was sent to the Paso Robles School for Boys.

In 1955, Buono married his high-school sweetheart, Geraldine Vinal, who was 17 years old at the time, who he had impregnated; however, less than a week later he left her. She would later give birth to a son, Michael Lee Buono, on 10 January 1956. Buono filed for divorce and refused to pay child support or let his son call him "Dad". He was back in jail for car theft when his first son was born.

Later, he impregnated Mary Castillo who gave birth to his second son, Angelo Anthony Buono III, at the end of 1956 and then married her in 1957. The couple would have four more children: Peter in 1957, Danny in 1958, Louis in 1960, and Grace in 1962. In 1964, Buono was believed to have sexually assaulted his two-year-old daughter Grace; however, there is insufficient literature to know fully the circumstances of the allegation. Buono's second marriage to Castillo also ended in divorce that same year after she purported that he had been physically, emotionally, and sexually abusive toward her. In a last-ditch effort to reconcile with him, Castillo was "rewarded" with his handcuffing her and threatening to kill her at gunpoint. Castillo would later recount a night during the first year they were together where Buono tied her spread-eagled to the bedposts and "raped her so violently she was afraid that he was going to kill her" and "her pain seemed to him his greatest pleasure" and, thus, he had no qualms of hurting her and didn't seem to care that the children witnessed the abuse. He avoided paying child support again.

Buono married a third time in 1965 to a 25-year-old single mother named Nannette Campino and the couple had two children of their own: Tony in 1967 and Sam in 1969. Despite being treated as poorly as Mary Castillo had been, Campino feared for her life on a daily basis but stayed until he began to sexually abuse her 14-year-old daughter. Buono allegedly bragged that he raped his stepdaughter because "[s]he needs breaking in" and then turned her over to his sons for their pleasure. Campino finally took her children, filed for divorce, and fled the state in 1971.

Buono, again, was arrested for auto theft and was sentenced to one year in prison; however, due to his large family his sentence was suspended so he could work to support them.

Buono married yet again, on a whim, to a woman named Deborah Taylor; however, the couple did not live together, nor did they ever divorce.

In 1975, he became a car upholsterer and purchased his own place at 703 E. Colorado Street to live and work. Despite his abuse, cockiness, overbearing nature, and lack of good looks, Buono was considered very attractive by women, particularly younger ones who were usually naïve about sex so it was easy to convince them that his outrageous demands and proclivities were normal. Thus, he frequently forced women to engage in sex acts with him and began a relationship with a teenage girl whom he twice impregnated.

He was ugly inside and out; very coarse, vulgar, ignorant, selfish, and sadistic.

Bianchi and Buono Together

At the age of 41, Buono came into contact with his cousin Kenneth Bianchi, the latter who, in 1975, moved to California and in with his cousin. Bianchi found his older cousin with "dyed black hair, gold chains around his neck, a large gaudy turquoise ring on his finger, red silk underwear and a virtual harem of jailbait girls". Buono taught Bianchi how to use fake police badges in order to coerce free sex from prostitutes. When they needed money the two also became pimps for a short time until the two girls who worked for them—Sabra Hannan and Becky Spears—escaped after enduring relentless abuse by Buono. Bianchi, still desiring to become a police officer, applied for jobs at the Los Angeles Sheriff's and Glendale Police Departments but neither were hiring. He then procured employment with a title company and used his first paycheck on an apartment and a Cadillac, moving in with coworker Kelli Boyd. Boyd rejected his marriage proposal as she considered Bianchi to be very jealous, immature, and a liar; however, in May 1977 she told him she was expecting their first child together. The couple moved to an apartment at 1950 Tamarind Avenue in Hollywood.

Bianchi also rented some office space and set himself up as a psychologist with a fake degree and credentials. He did not have many clients and when Boyd found out she was outraged. During the "Hillside Strangler" investigation, Bianchi told Boyd he had lung cancer and was undergoing chemotherapy and radiation to explain for his work absences; however, this was a lie. One day, detectives came to his apartment to ask questions but were "favorably impressed" and did not consider him a suspect at that time.

The Murders

In October 1977, the two men committed their first murder together. Their M.O. was to cruise around Los Angeles and use fake badges to convince women that they were undercover police officers. After persuading them into Buono's car that the men said was an unmarked police car, the two would take their victims to Buono's house where they would rape, torture, and strangle them with their "signature" weapon—a garrote (a handheld ligature such as a chain, rope, or strap)—although some of their victims were reportedly killed by lethal injection, electric shock, and gas asphyxiation. Their bodies were thus disposed of outside, frequently in hilly areas.

Yolanda Washington, 19

19-year-old tall, leggy, African-American prostitute Yolanda Washington disappeared on 17 October 1977 from Cathedral City, California. She was found the next day dumped just outside Forest Lawn Cemetery, beaten, raped, and strangled with a piece of cloth. Her corpse was cleaned and there were faint marks around her wrists, ankles, and neck. Her body was posed in a grotesque sexual position.

Judith Lynn Miller, 15

On 31 October, 15-year-old Judith Lynn Miller, a runaway, was found in a La Crescenta-Montrose neighborhood, face up on a parkway in a residential area. The homeowner covered her with a tarp so that neighborhood children wouldn't see her. After the incident, that same homeowner relocated his family to another state.

The victim was small and thin, perhaps 90 pounds, with medium length reddish-brown hair. She had bruising around her neck. She had also been raped and sodomized and her body had been posed with her legs in a diamond-like position.

Los Angeles Sheriff's Department Sergeant Frank Salerno was called to the site. He noticed insect activity upon her skin and on her eyelid was "a small piece of light-colored fluff" that he saved for forensic experts. He surmised that she had been killed elsewhere and her body had been deliberately placed where it would quickly be found.

At her autopsy, the coroner determined that she had been killed around midnight and was raped and sodomized.

There was no missing person's report matching this latest victim so after a couple of days, Salerno had the newspapers run a small story on her with a request to contact the police if anyone could identify her. Still nothing. Salerno then took her picture to Hollywood Boulevard and showed it to hundreds of runaways, addicts, homeless people, and prostitutes. The name Judy Miller kept coming up as a young destitute prostitute. One man named Markust Camden—a self-proclaimed bounty hunter—told Salerno that he saw Judy Miller leave the local fish and chips restaurant at 9:00 p.m. the night before she was found dead. In fact, he would pick Buono out of a police photo lineup, but failed to recognize Bianchi.

Eventually, Salerno was able to track down the Miller family and got a positive identification. They had nothing useful to contribute to the investigation.

Elissa "Lissa" Teresa Kastin, 21

Lissa Kastin, 21, was working as a waitress at the Healthfaire Restaurant to pay for ballet lessons as she was an avid dancer. She also worked part time for her father's real estate and construction business. She was last seen leaving work the night of 5 November. She was found the next day near the Chevy Chase Country Club in Glendale on 6 November; which was also near to where Buono lived. She had been beaten, raped, and strangled to death.

Salerno compared notes with the Glendale Police Department and noticed similarities between his latest victim and this new one. Both bodies had the same five-point ligature marks—ankles, wrists, and neck—and had been dumped within six miles of each other. This latest victim had been raped but there was no evidence of sodomy.

When Salerno looked at the dump site he was confident that at least two men were involved due to the large guardrail between the street and where the body was found and the near impossibility that one man could have gotten her body over it alone.

Dolores Cepeda, 12 and Sonja Johnson, 14

After their early murders failed to attract much publicity, Bianchi and Buono decided to find some younger victims.

12-year-old Dolores Cepeda and 14-year-old Sonja Johnson were abducted in Highland Park, California, on 13 November.

They had last been seen getting off a school bus heading home from St. Ignatius School and approaching a large two-tone sedan that, reportedly, had two men inside.

Both young girls were found on 20 November in the hills between Glendale and Eagle Rock, near Dodger Stadium by a young nine-year-old boy who was treasure hunting in the trash on the hillside.

Los Angeles Police Department Homicide Detective Dudley Varney had been called to this site.

Kristina Weckler, 20

That same day, 20-year-old Kristina Weckler was found on the other side of the same hillside where Cepeda and Johnson were found.

Weckler was a quiet, loving, and serious honors student at the Pasadena Art Center of Design and lived in Glendale.

She was found nude, raped, tortured, and strangled to death as evidenced by ligature marks on her neck, as well as around her wrists and ankles. She had blood oozing from her rectum and bruises on her breasts. Weckler was the first victim to show additional overt signs of torture; having been injected with Windex glass cleaner she had oozing injection marks on her arms.

Los Angeles Police Department Homicide Detective Sergeant Bob Grogan—Varney's partner—was called to this site. He noticed that there was no indication of any disturbance of the foliage in the area or evidence that the body had been dragged there. Grogan made a mental note that she likely had been killed elsewhere and then carried and dumped in this location by one or maybe two men.

At this point, police were entertaining the idea that there was more than one killer and that they were becoming increasingly more sadistic.

Jane Evelyn King, 28

28-year-old actress Jane King disappeared in Los Angeles around 10 November 1977, and was found near the Los Feliz off ramp of the Golden State Freeway on 23 November. She had been sodomized and strangled and her body was badly decomposed. After King was found, Los Angeles Police Department officials—in addition to Glendale Police Department and Los Angeles County Sheriff's Department officers—created a task force to catch the "Hillside Strangler".

Lauren Rae Wagner, 18

18-year-old student Lauren Wagner lived with her parents in the San Fernando Valley. Her parents had gone to bed on 28 November, expecting their daughter to return home before midnight. The next morning, they found her car parked across the street with the door ajar.

Wagner was found later that day in a wooded area near Glendale's Mount Washington area. She was lying partially in the street, nude, with ligature marks on her ankles, wrists, and neck. Wagner, too, had been tortured as the palms of her hands contained several burn marks.

At the dump site was also a "shiny track of some sticky liquid, which had attracted a convoy of ants". Police considered that if the substance was saliva or semen from the killer then, perhaps, his blood type could be determined, as tests on semen found inside the earlier victims revealed nothing. It was later found that Bianchi was not a secretor, in that his blood type could not be determined by other bodily fluids. DNA testing had not come into popularity at this time.

When Wagner's father questioned the neighbors, it turned out that the woman who lived in the house where his daughter's car was parked, Beulah Stofer, saw Wagner's abduction. Stofer said that Wagner had pulled over to the curb at around 9:00 p.m. and two men had parked their car beside hers. After some type of disagreement, Wagner "ended up in the car with the two men".

When Grogan went to talk to the neighbor, she told him that she had just had a phone call from a man with a New York accent who told her to "keep her mouth shut about what she had witnessed or he would kill her". Stofer also told Grogan that the car was a large dark sedan with a white top and that one of the men dragged Wagner from her car into his while Wagner protested, "You won't get away with this!" Stofer described one man as tall and young with acne scars while the other was older and shorter, Latin-looking, and with bushy hair. She said she was positive that she would identify them again. This statement rang true when she picked both Bianchi and Buono out of a photo lineup shown to her by Grogan.

Kimberly Diane Martin, 17

Tall, blonde prostitute Kimberly Martin, 17, disappeared from Echo Park, California, and was found strangled to death on 13 December 1977 on a steep hillside on Alvarado Street. Martin had worked for the Climax "modeling agency".

Police believed they had two reasonably good leads in this case. First, Martin's last "client" called her to 1950 Tamarind, apartment 114; however, this turned out to be a vacant apartment. Secondly, the murderer called from a payphone in the lobby of the Hollywood Public Library on Ivar Street. Unfortunately, nothing came from these leads.

Cindy Lee Hudspeth, 20

On 16 February 1978, 20-year-old Bible school teacher and secretary at an Echo Park church Cindy Hudspeth was found in the trunk of her bright orange 1977 Datsun B210 that had been pushed over a cliff on Angeles Crest in Los Angeles National Forest near La Canada. She had been raped and strangled, with the strangulation marks similar to those associated with the "Hillside Strangler".

Hudspeth was also a neighbor of Weckler even though the two women did not know each other. Interestingly, Bianchi also lived in the same apartment complex; however, this lead was never pursued even though both Grogan and Salerno believed that there was a good chance that at least one of the murderers lived in the Glendale area.

After this case, the lack of additional victims resulted in the disbanding of the "Hillside Strangler" Task Force.

Jill Barcomb, 18 (originally believed to be a Hillside Strangler victim)

18-year-old prostitute Jill Barcomb was abducted in Beverly Hills and found near the famous Hollywood sign on 9 November. Whereas it was originally believed that she was a victim of the "Hillside Strangler" because she had been raped, beaten, and strangled, in 2005, her death was conclusively proven through DNA analysis to have been committed by Rodney Alcala, the "Dating Game Killer".

Also, sometime in 1977, the two men gave Catharine Lorre a ride with the intent of killing her; however, when they learned that she was the daughter of famous actor Peter Lorre who played a child murderer in Fritz Lang's 1931 masterpiece film M, they let her go. She had no idea who the men were until they were arrested.

The two stopped killing after their ninth victim, Hudspeth (although at this time it was presumed they had ten victims with Barcomb), likely due to the birth of Bianchi's son and, as some surmise, that he had made some acquaintances within the Los Angeles Police Department who would take him on ride-alongs around the city, ironically, looking for the killers, and Bianchi could talk about nothing else while in police presence. On the night they had tried to abduct another victim, the two men got into a heated argument when Bianchi told his cousin that he had been questioned in the "Hillside Strangler" case. After Bianchi's confession about being questioned by police, Buono, furious, threatened to kill his cousin.

Bianchi's Washington Murders

Bianchi's girlfriend, Kelli Boyd gave birth to their son, Sean, in February 1978, and in March Boyd decided to return to her parents in Bellingham, Washington, as she was tired of both Los Angeles and Bianchi's lifestyle. After three months of pleading to be reunited, Boyd relented and Bianchi moved to Washington in May. Bianchi's role as boyfriend and father was relatively successful and he even took a job as a security guard, ultimately earning the trust of his supervisors. However, this way of life did little to alleviate Bianchi's murderous urges. Within six months he was actively looking for new victims.

On 11 January 1978, Bianchi lured two Western Washington University students—roommates Karen Mandic, 22, and Diane Wilder, 27—to a house he allegedly "guarded" under the pretense of housesitting. Once there, he raped, tortured, and murdered them.

On 12 January, police were informed that two female students were missing after Mandic's boss became worried that she didn't arrive at work that day. He did remember that she had told him she had accepted a housesitting job in a wealthy Bayside neighborhood from a security guard friend of hers. When former-priest-turned-Bellingham-Police-Chief Terry Mangan went to the girls' home he found a hungry cat, as well as the address of the home where they were to housesit. The name of one security guard kept coming up, as well as a record that Bianchi had used a company truck that same night, supposedly to take into the shop for repairs. This never happened. Mangan began to consider the fact that the women had met with foul play.

Police then went to the Bayside house and found a wet footprint. They also interviewed a neighbor who told them that a security guard asked her to check on the house except for the night the women disappeared because "there was special work being done to the alarm system and he didn't want her to be taken as an intruder".

After a press conference, a woman called police to report that a car had been abandoned near her home in a heavily-wooded area. In the car were the bodies of Mandic and Wilder. Both had bruising and had been strangled to death.

Mangan had the security guard picked up. He gave them no trouble. His name was Kenneth Bianchi.

There was ample forensic evidence in this case; most notably foreign pubic hairs on the girls and fibers from the house's carpet matching fibers on the dead girls' clothing and shoes. Additionally, when police searched Bianchi's home they found several items stolen from job sites where he worked.

Remembering back to the "Hillside Strangler" cases in Los Angeles—and knowing Bianchi had lived there—Mangan called the police departments in California who had worked on the task force. He spoke to Detective Frank Salerno to whom everything finally made sense. Detectives tirelessly worked to link Bianchi to the strangler cases and were confident that he was one of the murderers.

Investigation and Arrest

Bianchi was not as careful this time, having left significant clues, most notably his car with California license plates was seen and subsequently connected to the addresses of two Hillside Strangler victims. Without mastermind Buono, Bianchi didn't have the wherewithal to cover his tracks.

Bianchi was arrested the following day, on 12 January 1979.

Buono was arrested on 22 October 1979, after Bianchi told police about his cousin's complicity in the murders.

Trial and Conviction

Prior to his 1981 trial, Bianchi decided to plead not guilty by reason of insanity and claimed to have a separate personality named "Steve Walker" who had committed the murders. After several interviews by experts specializing in multiple personality disorder and hypnosis, it was determined that he was faking. Immediately after Dr. Martin Orne mentioned to Bianchi that in genuine cases of multiple personality disorder there are typically at least three personalities, Bianchi created another alter ego named "Billy", shortly followed by two more. It was later determined that the name "Steven Walker" came from a student whose identity Bianchi had previously tried to steal to enable him to fraudulently practice psychology. Further, in Bianchi's apartment investigators found several psychology books which laid credence to Bianchi's ability to fake the disorder. He was eventually diagnosed with antisocial personality disorder with sexual sadism.

During trial, there was significant physical trace evidence against the two men; including fibers from Buono's upholstery from his home and workshop on two of the victims; an imprint of a fake police badge on his wallet; and hairs from rabbits he had raised on another victim.

Bianchi agreed to plead guilty and testify against his cousin in order to get leniency, albeit uncooperatively (evidence of his passive-aggressive personality disorder).

Judge Ronald M. George—who would later become California Supreme Court Chief Justice—said during Buono's sentencing hearing, "I would not have the slightest reluctance to impose the death penalty in this case were it within my power to do so. Ironically, although these two defendants utilized almost every form of legalized execution against their victims, the defendants have escaped any form of capital punishment." On an interesting side note, George's roommate at the time was author Darcy O'Brien who, four years after the trial, wrote a book about the case.

Both men were sentenced to life in prison.

While incarcerated, Buono married mother-of-three Christine Kizuka in 1986 while she was visiting her husband—and father of her children—who was in the cell next door to Buono at the Los Angeles County Jail, serving 18 months for assault with a deadly weapon. She worked as a supervisor at the California State Employment Development Department.

Whereas the 64-year-old Bianchi continues to serve his life sentence at the Washington State Penitentiary in Walla Walla, Buono died of a heart attack on 21 September 2002 while serving life at Calipatria State Prison in Calipatria, California. Denied for parole on 18 August 2010, Bianchi will next be eligible for parole in 2025.

Aftermath

Bianchi is also a suspect in the "Alphabet Murders"—also known as the "Double Initial Murders"—which occurred in the early 1970s in his hometown of Rochester wherein three young girls were raped, strangled to death, and dumped in the wilderness. At the time he worked as an ice cream vendor situated near two of the murder sites. On 16 November 1971, ten-year-old Carmen Colon disappeared and was found two days later in Churchville, New York, 12 miles from where she was last seen. 11-year-old Wanda Walkowicz disappeared on 2 April 1973 and was found the next day in Webster, New York, off State Route 104, seven miles from Rochester. Finally, on 26 November 1973, Michelle Maenza, 11, disappeared and was found two days later in Macedon, New York, a mere 15 miles from Rochester. They were called the "Alphabet Murders" because not only did the young victims have the same initial for their first and last name but they were also found in cities which began with the same letter.

Whereas Bianchi has repeatedly tried to get his name cleared from these murders he remains a suspect because his vehicle was seen near two of the murder sites.

Another series of murders with similar circumstances occurred in California in the late 1970s and investigators have hypothesized that they are connected to the Rochester "Alphabet Murders". In 1977, Roxene Roggasch, Paula Parsons, and Carmen Colon (like one of the original "Alphabet Murder" victims) were found raped and dead. Whereas Bianchi was tried for six murders, DNA exonerated him of the California "Alphabet Murders".

A 2008 movie entitled The Alphabet Killer was very loosely based upon the murders, and in 2010 a book written by Cheri Farnsworth called Alphabet Killer: The True Story of the Double Initial Murders was released.

In 1980, Bianchi started a relationship with a Veronica Lynn Compton, who was a defense witness during his trial. Compton, a cocaine addict who was fascinated by serial killers, was working as a scriptwriter in Hollywood. On one of her numerous visits with Bianchi while he was incarcerated, she gave him a copy of her screenplay entitled The Mutilated Cutter, about a female serial killer, and asked for this input. Compton grew increasingly fixated and allegedly fell in love with Bianchi. Later, she was convicted and incarcerated for attempting to strangle a cocktail waitress who she had lured to a hotel in a ploy to have the world—and authorities—believe that the real "Hillside Strangler" was still on the loose and that the wrong man was incarcerated. To make it look like an authentic "Hillside Strangler" murder, Bianchi manipulated and used Compton as a means to get out of prison by giving her semen of his smuggled out of the facility in a rubber glove to plant on the body. Despite that DNA forensics had not been utilized at that time, semen could still be analyzed to demonstrate the killer's blood type; however, Bianchi was not a secretor. The intended victim managed to get away and Compton was tried and convicted of first-degree attempted murder and sentenced to life. Compton was paroled from prison in 2003.

In 1992, Bianchi sued Catherine Yronwode for $8.5 million for putting an image of his face on a trading card. He claimed his face was his trademark. The case was dismissed with the judge saying that if Bianchi's face was, indeed, his trademark during the murders then he would not have tried to hide it from police.

In 2007, Buono's grandson, Christopher Buono, shot his grandmother—Mary Castillo who was married to Buono at one time—and then committed suicide. Christopher was unaware of his grandfather's true identity until 2005.

Bianchi and Buono are immortalized in film. The 1989 film The Case of the Hillside Stranglers—based on O'Brien's book—starred Dennis Farina as Buono and Billy Zane as Bianchi. In the 2004 film The Hillside Strangler, Buono was portrayed by actor Nicholas Turturro and Bianchi was portrayed by C. Thomas Howell.

The 2006 movie Rampage: The Hillside Strangler Murders starred Tomas Arana as Buono and Clifton Collins, Jr. as Bianchi.

In 2001 the Discovery Channel aired an episode of The New Detectives that revisited the murders.

Bianchi and Buono have also been mentioned several times on the television show Criminal Minds as an example of killer teams with psychopathic predatory sexual sadist personalities who murdered their victims together.

ROADSIDE STRANGLER

67

JASMINE GREY

When one envisions a serial killer, they think of a cold, calculating, heartless monster. As humans, some of us have developed ways to recognize other humans that are looking to cause us harm. If we look at a mug shot of famous another serial killer, like Charles Manson or Jeffery Dahmer, one could say that these men "look" like serial killers. Maybe it's because of their wild eyes, the way that they hold themselves, or the "creepy" feeling one receives from their presence. These factors are enough to make a person stay as far away from the killer as possible, but sadly, not all predators come with a warning sign. Michael Bruce Ross, later to be known as the Roadside Strangler, was a ruthless predator that slipped under the radars of the multiple women that he attacked, raped, and murdered. Detective Malchik, Ross' arresting officer, described this serial killer as, "There was nothing threatening about him, there was no signal to any of these people that there was a dark side or something that they should be afraid of. He was able to conceal that until it became time for him to attack these innocent, young women." Ross seemed to be an average-looking man of completely average-strength and abilities, but underneath his calm and normal exterior beat the heart of a man who struggled with his sadistic, sexual compulsions. When someone spoke to Michael Ross, they would say that he put off a very friendly and articulate demeanor seemed very well educated and kind, but it was merely a costume that he had created over a lifetime. The creepy part about Michael Ross, despite how honest and upfront he is about his murders, is the mystery behind his words. Is he being genuine or is this merely an act? Is he being honest or are we being deceived? His state of mind drifts from monotone claims to not possess any remorse for his monstrosities to genuine pleas for a chemical castration to reduce his perverse sexual desires. Michael Bruce Ross' case was a strange one, to say the least, and his mental condition will forever be remembered as a very dark part in Connecticut history.

The Childhood

Michael Bruce Ross was born on July 26, 1959. Among three other children, Michael Bruce Ross was born into the life of a middle-class chicken farmer. His mother Pat was impregnated in high school and forced into a shotgun marriage with Michael's father, Dan Ross. Needless to say, they did not go on to lead a very happy marriage. Pat Ross was a very mentally unstable woman, who underwent two abortions and was institutionalized twice. She abandoned her children and family once to run off with another man, but she soon returned to a depressing and emotionally unhealthy life on the farm. Pat Ross seemed to resent Michael more than the other children. His sister claimed that Michael received the brunt of their mother's aggression. Michael Ross claimed that he didn't remember his dark childhood or his emotional abuse-ridden family; he only had fond memories of working on his father's farm. The joyous memories of working on the farm centered on his peculiar job; Michael's job was to ring the necks of sick and malnourished chickens.

He recalled that he began to experience sexual fantasies around this time, like most boys his age, but they weren't anything like the hellish compulsions he faced in his adulthood. He explained his boyish daydreams as non-violent, although they might've been considered peculiar by most. In an interview, Michael describes his early, innocent fantasies of women, "I would kidnap women and take them to my safe place, and then they would fall in love with me, and never want to leave." It has been said that Michael was molested as a child by his mentally ill uncle while babysitting. As an adult, Michael Ross claimed that he did not remember this incident or his uncle at all; Michael was only six years old when the suspected uncle committed suicide. Whether Michael was too young to recall the incident or if he merely repressed the memory, the irreparable damage that comes along with molestation could be a very influential part of Michael's slip into sexual sadism. Despite his strange desires, his dysfunctional family, and his history of abuse, Michael was considered to be a pretty average child. As a teenager, he excelled in school, graduating as number sixteen in his high school class, and he eventually moved to Cornell University to study Agriculture and Life Sciences.

College Years

He continued to excel academically throughout his years at university. He studied Economics, Agriculture, and Life Sciences, and excelled in all of his academic endeavors. He joined the FFA (Future Farmers of America) and the Alpha Zeta fraternity. Ross' sophomore year roommate and Alpha Zeta brother, described Ross in 1977, "He kind of followed his own drum and went his own way." Michael never made any real connections in his fraternity, nor did he really make connections to anyone besides the long string of girls that he dated. In his college year, Michael Ross was rarely without a girlfriend, and he was rarely thinking about anything but. "There was always a certain obsession on his part regarding women," said his Alpha Zeta roommate, "That seemed to be such a big issue, a constant topic—needing a woman, needing to have a girlfriend. He would be obsessed about the relationship."

Ross claims that he did not experience truly violent sexual fantasies until his years at Cornell University. He especially did not begin to fantasize about raping women until his sophomore year in college. Michael Ross said that somewhere in his undergraduate years, he began to embrace the desires that brewed within him. He started his downward spiral with a very small step. He began to stalk his fellow students on campus. He would follow close by, making it known that he was behind her. "I would get a thrill by them knowing that I was following them. That they would be scared and that gave me a thrill," Michael explained his early experimentation with his predatory nature. When simply stalking the women wasn't enough, Michael eventually turned to towards rape. He hid in the bushes of Beebe Lake and raped a visiting student. Later, he attempted to rape another girl outside of the school observatory but failed. These assaults were only stepping stones to the full-fledged horror that Michael Ross was destined to cause. During his senior year at Cornell University, Michael Ross met Dzung Ngoc Tu, a Vietnamese student, and his very first murder victim.

The case of Dzung Ngoc Tu perplexed officials everywhere. She was found on May 17, 1981, in the Fall Creek Gorge. She died from a skull fracture and her body laid there for five days until she was discovered. It appeared to be a suicide, as if she had jumped from the bridge overhead and hit her head upon the fall, but there was no suicide note left at the scene. Close friends and family of Dzung Ngoc Tu claimed that there absolutely no signs of suicidal tendencies when she was alive and investigators found absolutely no reason for killing herself. Her body showed no signs of sexual abuse, there were no suspects, and the police had no idea that the culprit was actually Michael Ross, a man who was only connected to her by their similar majors. The case went cold when the police couldn't find a suspect. It wasn't until Michael Ross was already in prison for the murders and rapes of four other women when he confessed to murdering and raping a Vietnamese girl that went to his school in New York.

The Attacks and Murders of The Roadside Strangler

Michael Ross chose his victims merely off of chance and circumstance. If he encountered a woman that was in a vulnerable position, he felt this undeniable compulsion to attack. "There's nothing they could've said or done. It was me, it wasn't them," Michael Ross admitted with a solemn tone of voice, years after his final attack, "They were dead as soon as I saw them, I think."

Michael claimed that he only attacked women to relieve pressure that built up from his personal relationships with the women in his life. When he was working in North Carolina, shortly after he graduated from college, Michael recalled that he had a very difficult visit from his fiancé, which caused him to attack a random woman shortly after he dropped his fiancé off at the airport. He noticed a woman walking on the sidewalk with a baby stroller, so Michael pulled the car over and attacked her, using her own child as a weapon. "I told her that if she didn't do what I wanted, I would smash the baby's head against the wall of the house," Michael described in an interview, he seemed as if he were on the verge of tears, "I've always said that I never understood why these women never really resisted me. I'm not a big, strong guy, but nobody ever seemed to fight. I've always just contributed it as I must say something like that, or similar to it, to the other victims." He raped and strangled the woman, then left her for dead in her driveway.

On June 15, 1982, a 23-year-old woman named Debra Smith Taylor was attacked by Michael Ross in a park. He pulled her over where no one could see them, raped her, and forced her to roll over on her stomach; he then strangled her from behind. The young girl's body was discovered much later in a dried up river bed, only a few miles away from the location of another of Ross' victims, Tammy L. Williams. "Each time I killed, I made myself believe that I wasn't going to kill again," Michael Ross explained in an interview. It wasn't very long before he killed again.

His next attack occurred on a cold Thanksgiving Day in 1983. Michael Ross encountered Robin Stavinsky outside of Norwich State Hospital. He saw the woman in a vulnerable position and he took advantage of the situation. He forced the 19-year-old girl into a wooded area and demanded her to remove her clothing. Ross forced himself on the young girl then told her to roll over on her stomach. He strangled her from behind until the innocent Robin

Stavinksky died in his hands. "Serial killers like to strangle their victims and that is, I guess, the most common form of killing because there's more of a connection there. It's more real and it's not as quick," Michael Ross explained why he enjoyed strangling so much. After he was finished with her, he covered her body with leaves and left her for dead.

The Roadside Strangler struck again on Easter Sunday, 1984. April Brunias and Leslie Shelly were hitchhiking on the side of the road when Michael Ross happened to drive their way. He pulled over and offered the young girls a ride. The girls did not find Ross threatening so they got into his car and asked him to drop them off at the next gas station. When Michael passed the gas station, one of the girls drew a kitchen knife and threatened to stab him. In an interview Michael Ross explained what happened next, "I almost drove off of the road, I was so surprised. I don't know what I said, but I said something and she gave the knife to me. It obviously scared her." He parked the car at Beach Pond and used a cloth to bound both of the girls by their hands and feet. He put Leslie Shelly in the trunk of his car, then dragged the girl named April a few feet away from the car. He raped the young girl, flipped her over onto her stomach, and strangled her until she died. He then took Leslie out of the trunk and did the same thing to her. "The smallest one, Leslie Shelly, has always bothered me more than the others. I think it was because she was so small, I think it was because she was so cooperative, and I think it was because the way she was killed was so close to the fantasy. That was the one that was… it was like it was fantasy," Michael explained. The girls were only fourteen years old when they were murdered.

It was a summer afternoon, around three o'clock on June 13, 1984, when the Roadside Strangler committed the murder that would finally get him caught. He was driving home from work when he passed Wendy Baribeault, who was walking down the side of busy Route 12 in Libson, only a few miles away from his home. Michael Ross pulled the car over and began to speak to this 17-year-old girl; he repeatedly invited her to his company picnic. After a little bit of conversation, Michael forced the beautiful, young girl over a stone wall and into the woods. "When I attacked her, I don't believe that I was in control. I don't think I would've been able to stop," Michael Ross explained his mental state during this attack, "I didn't really feel anything. I knew what was going on and I saw what was going on, but it was more like watching an old film..." Michael then raped the innocent girl and strangled her, just like the others, then entombed her in the stone wall that lined the busy road. The road was so busy, in fact, that there were several eyewitnesses to the attack.

The Investigation of the Roadside Strangler

The police had absolutely no leads on the murderer (a.k.a. The Roadside Strangler) that had taken Connecticut by storm. That was until Wendy Baribeault's body was found. There were dozens of eye witnesses to her attack and composite drawings were created that matched the facial features of local Michael Bruce Ross. Witnesses also noted that the attacker was driving a blue Toyota. Michael Malchik, the investigator assigned to the case, compiled a list of several thousand blue Toyotas. This tiny bit of evidence eventually led investigators directly to Ross' house, which was only three miles away from the location of the crime scene. Michael allegedly dropped hints that he was the murderer upon speaking to the police. "It all had to end," Michael Ross explained. It wasn't long before Michael was called into an interview with police in 1984. After a few hours of grueling interrogation, Michael Bruce Ross confessed to all crimes that he'd committed in Connecticut, but left out the murders in New York. "It's a mystery to me to this day, but it's typical of him," stated Detective Malchik, "Here he is, confessing to six murders, and he thought enough ahead not to tell us about the New York ones. Looking back at it, it's obvious he was thinking of something. He was always thinking two steps ahead. He's got his own agenda, but I couldn't for the life of me tell you what it is."

When Michael confessed to the murders, he seemed very sorrowful and remorseful, but he claimed not to feel a blink of remorse, "I don't want to say that I don't have any remorse, it's just like they weren't real..." Michael explains his feelings towards hid victims in a later interview, "I can't see them as I was killing them, so when I say I don't have any remorse, that doesn't mean that I don't have any regrets, or wish that didn't happen, or there was something that I could do to bring them back or anything – I don't have any feelings towards them. I feel like I should be tormented by them - by what they look like when I was killing them – or tormented by what was happening immediately before I killed them – but none of that's there. None of that's there at all."

"The only time he said he was sorry, was that he was sorry for getting caught," Michael's arresting officer explained, "He (Michael Ross) told me matter-of-factly, he said, 'If you hadn't caught me, I would've just kept on killing, again.'" This eerie statement by itself was enough to put the Roadside Strangler to death immediately, but his strange nature kept investigators questioning his motives behind being so upfront and honest about his heinous crimes. Did he secretly want to get caught? Was this all part of some big plot to instill his insanity?

Anne Cournoyer, Michael's correction counselor, described his mannerisms as he spoke of the horrible crimes that he committed, "One minute he's very, you know, looks like he on the verge of crying, and the next minute he's sort of giggling nervously - or sadistically – you just really don't know. You think that maybe, it's out of nervousness, but he could be getting pleasure out of talking about it."

A full-scale investigation of Michael Bruce Ross' life led to the realization of his wavering mental stability. Michael Ross explained that he could never recall the faces of his victims, even directly after the murders, "You'd think that if you killed someone, you would have the face imprinted in your mind and that you wouldn't be able to get it out of your mind – I don't have that. I never had that," He explained, "The only faces I could see was what was in the newspapers a few days later when they were missing. You know, the high school pictures and 'anybody know where this girl is?' type of thing. When I think of them, that's the picture that I see. I don't see them as they were when I killed them. If you had stopped me right after and gave me a composite drawing of like twelve pictures - you know - some blondes, brunettes, whatever – I wouldn't have been able to pick them out. Even immediately after I killed them."

The names of all eight women were: Dzung Ngoc Tu (25), Paula Perrera (16), Tammy Williams (17), Debra Smith Taylor (23), Robin Stavinksy (19), April Brunias (14), Leslie Shelley (14), and Wendy Baribeault (17). He was only charged with the murders of the four Connecticut women because the murders of Dzung Ngoc Tu and Paula Perrera took place in New York. He was sentenced to death on July 6, 1987, but remained on death row for eighteen years after his sanity was called into question.

The Curious Case of Michael Bruce Ross

Michael spent the next eighteen years of his life caught in a battle of the Connecticut justice system. In court, a team of psychiatrists flocked to the defense of Mr. Michael Ross. After a parade of psychiatric evaluation, Michael was deemed mentally unwell, due to his dark childhood and his undeniable compulsions. Dr. Fred Berlin, the well-known co-founder of the Johns Hopkins Sexual Disorder Clinic, testified that Ross was struggling with a mental disorder called sexual sadism. Meaning that he gained sexual excitement from the pain and suffering of others. This discovery alone was not enough to save Ross' life, but Michael's claim to lose all self-control during the murders was enough to set back his execution date. Connecticut's state psychiatrist reluctantly agreed that Ross was not mentally capable enough to be responsible for his own actions, and therefore, it was not right to put him to death. Dr. Robert Miller wrote in a private letter, "I can't see how I could testify against psychopathology playing a sufficient role in defendant's behavior." Although this letter was never presented in court, Michael Ross' death sentence was overturned in 1994 and a new sentencing hearing was scheduled in 2000.

Michael Bruce Ross spent most of his time on death row writing about the mental disorder that took hold of his entire life. Michael claimed to have no control over his actions due to his compulsions. He described his sexual sadism as "a mental illness that drove me to rape and kill" and "made me physically unable to control my actions." During his time in prison, Michael still fell victim to his compulsions. It was impossible for him to control his sexual desires, so he spent the first few months of his incarceration reliving the murders. He claimed that he would fantasize these murders over and over again, hurting himself and causing sores from compulsive masturbation. It wasn't very long before he begged for some type of relief from his sexual desires, which came in the form of chemical castration. Ross was given medication that was designed to lower his testosterone levels and it finally relieved him from his sadistic compulsions. Thanks to this medication, Michael Bruce Ross was finally able to think clearly and he was able to see the true nature of his crimes.

The team of prosecutors naturally disagreed with the defense's attempts to lessen his blame. Prosecutors claimed that if he were unable to control his desires, he would've made less calculated attacks. It was reasonable to assume that Ross experienced these sexual desires constantly, which means that he probably experienced these feelings while in public places, or places where his actions could've been seen and reprimanded. Instead, Ross chose his victims very carefully, only acting when the girls were vulnerable and alone. Disproving the defenses' claims more so was the fact that Ross' hid their bodies after the attack, which further strengthened his blame and the case that he knew precisely what he was doing when he was doing it. "I'm not saying I wasn't there or it was multi-personality or any of that type of crap," Michael Ross later explained the strange fog he experienced while he murdered these innocent women, "I was there and I did it, but I wasn't one hundred percent there." To set light upon Mr. Michael Ross' guilt, Prosecutors relied on the "Policeman at the Elbow" test: would

Ross have committed the crime even if a policeman had been standing next to him?

The defense team immediately disagreed with the statement that all of Ross' attacks were calculated and well thought out, considering the murder of Ms. Wendy B. who was murdered next to a busy road with several eyewitnesses, "When I attacked her, I don't believe I was in control. I don't think I could've stopped." Michael spoke about the murder that eventually resulted in his incarnation. "Could he control himself? Well, two juries rejected that," Detective Malchik recalls, "As the state's attorney said at the trial if Ross was so out of control, why didn't he just rape the girl in between the yellow lines of Route 12? He made it simple for the juries to understand."

John Blume, a professor at the Law school and co-founder of the Cornell Death Penalty Project, noted the how the jury in Ross' case did not take the opinions of the psychological experts seriously. "The thing that's disturbing," Professor Blume stated, "is that even when the experts all say your client is insane, juries will still reject it." Despite the team of psychologists on Ross' side, claiming that he was completely unable to stop himself from committing these monstrosities, the jury chose not to believe them.

Somewhere in the eighteen years of Michael Ross' incarceration, he decided that he did not deserve to live anymore. Shortly after Michael wrote a story called "It's Time for Me to Die", he reconnected with a woman named Kathy Jaeger, who served as his pastoral advocate that converted Ross to Catholicism. Ross wrote in a newsletter that Jaeger, "was able to breach my defenses and was able to touch my soul as no one else ever has." He later called Ms. Kathy Jaeger "the most important woman in my life" and claimed that "If I were a free man, I would ask her to marry me." Although Kathy rejects his claims to romance, she continued to support Michael Ross throughout his decisions.

After she entered Michael's life, there was a great shift in the nature of his case. Michael was done fighting for his life and the mental condition that wreaked havoc on his entire existence. After his original death sentence was overturned in 1994, the court ordered a new penalty hearing, but instead of going through the hearing with his public defenders, Ross acted as his own attorney. He worked with prosecutor C. Robert Satti to created what was deemed as "death pact" that allowed the imposition of the death penalty without a penalty hearing. "Please allow me to go into the courtroom . . . to accept the death penalty as punishment for my actions," Ross wrote in a letter to Satti. "I'm not asking you to do this for me, but for the families involved, who do not deserve to suffer further and who, in some small way, might gain a sense of peace of mind by these actions and my execution." The "death pact" was rejected by the judge as a "short cut" involving a human life, so Michael Ross flip-flopped back into his old ways. Ross returned to his defense team and reverted back into fighting for his life, claiming that his crimes were merely a product of his mental illness. He was resentenced to death soon after.

Jaeger said that Ross's sudden acceptance of death was a sincere attempt to provide closure for the families of his victims, "He told me, 'You know I don't want to do this. But I have to.' He just really felt anguish over what he had done. Really, really harsh anguish and self-loathing. Contrary to media reports, he doesn't want to die. He wishes that the justice system got it right years ago and gave him life sentences because he does have a mental illness. And the sad thing is, if they had done that, the families of his victims wouldn't have been re-victimized [by the ongoing appeals]. Michael is trying, in essence, to save them from any more of that."

Whether his acceptance of the death sentence was sincere, or not, Michael Bruce Ross was sentenced to death by lethal injection on May 13, 2005. He chose not to speak any last words before his death and died peacefully in the execution chair. Some family members believed that his death was too peaceful. Debbie Dupuis, Robin Stavinsky's sister, stated that she thought she would "feel closure" but instead just "felt anger" as she watched Ross simply lay there, go to sleep and die.

The state of Connecticut finally decided to end the life of the Roadside Strangler and put an end to the anguish that the families had to endure. After a very tragic and dark lifetime, Michael Bruce Ross and his sadistic compulsions were finally laid to rest.

Conclusion

Michael Bruce Ross is the type of cold, calculating, manipulative killer that we only read about in horror novels. His crimes almost seem too heartless and brutal to be true, but the victims of the Roadside Strangler would tell you that he is nothing but a cruel reality. In only a few years, Michael assaulted a countless number of women and murdered eight. Although he was only charged with four murders, Ross was forced to withstand eighteen long years of debate over his life sentence. In prison, he transitioned from a vicious killer who was truly non-remorseful for his brutal crimes to a man who seemed to genuinely regret his life choices and the pain that he subjected. Towards the end of his life, Ross begged for removal from his troubled existence, not only for himself but to end the long and grueling process of the legal system. Despite his transition into humanity, Michael Bruce Ross never took full blame for his actions. He flip-flopped between blaming his childhood, his compulsions, and his interpersonal relationships for these terrible crimes. He claimed to never feel any guilt or remorse for his actions, simply because he wasn't completely there while they were taking place. During these attacks, Michael claims that he was under some type of spell, some type of fog that completely disconnected him from his actions. He was completely able to murder and rape these innocent women without feeling guilt or remorse, or even being able to recall the very faces of his victims', only moments after their attack. Michael Ross was an extremely troubled man who suffered from a very extreme case of sexual sadism. Michael explained his cruel, heartless, attacks with vivid details and an undetached tone of voice. The scariest part about his calm demeanor is the monotone way that he described the way he stole the lives of these young, innocent women. He speaks as if he were not responsible for killing these beautiful and young women, although he willingly confesses to the murders. He claimed that he was merely a victim of his sexual compulsions since his college years and the women he attacked were merely in the wrong place at the wrong time. Whether his desires were really uncontrollable or if it was merely an excuse, Michael Bruce Ross' case remains to be one of the most perplexing cases in American history. His mere mental condition was enough to perplex the entire state of Connecticut – how could this well-spoken, articulate man with such a great personality, commit these terrible crimes? Why didn't anyone notice his decline and stop it? What was it that made this seemingly normal man snap into the Roadside Strangler? Although the answers to these questions are uncertain, they definitely are unnerving. Michael Ross was created by circumstances, by his dark upbringing, and a lifetime of people letting him slip through the cracks. Everyone saw him as an average, everyday college student, so no one thought to ask. The woman that he murdered were sadly only stepping stones into the downward spiral into his sickness and they were eventually caused the end of his vicious, murderous cycle.

STOCKWELL STRANGLER : The True Story of Kenneth Erskine

83

NATALIE MARSHALL

Kenneth Erskine, known as "The Stockwell Strangler" due to the geographic proximities of his murders, was a deeply troubled young man who had demonstrated worrisome signs of violence and schizophrenia from a young age. He was a gerontophile in that he had an unnatural sexual attraction to the elderly. Gerontophilia, essentially, is the opposite of pedophilia. Erskine would break into elderly men's and women's London flats and strangle them while they were in bed; after which he would rape and/or sodomize most of them. To demonstrate his own warped sense of love for his victims he would cross their arms across their chest, close their eyes, and tuck them into bed. Also, perhaps to hide his shame, he would turn his victims' family photographs face down. There was much speculation among mental health professionals that Erskine also suffered from schizophrenia from a very young age.

He was eventually convicted of seven murders and one attempted murder and sentenced to life in prison in 1988 at the age of 25. However, in July 2009, following an appeal his murder convictions were reduced to manslaughter on the grounds of diminished capacity and he received a hospital order to serve his life sentences at Broadmoor Hospital. While he has the potential to be granted parole in 2028, the trial judge's original order was that Erskine should spend at least 40 years behind bars, thus making him at least 65 years of age before potential eligibility for release.

Early Life

Kenneth Erskine was born in Hammersmith, London in July 1963. His mother Margaret was British and his father Charles was from Antigua. He was one of four boys, had an average IQ when tested at eight years old, and was remembered by neighbors to be a "chubby, Bible reading soul"; however, he became increasingly violent and difficult to control. For example, as a child, Erskine had tried to hang his younger brother, John, twice.

Erskine was then sent to a series of schools for maladjusted and troubled children where he received his formal education. He frequently and violently attacked his teachers and classmates and was identified as inhabiting a fantasy world with murderous impulses. In his own private fantasy world he would take on the role of Lawrence of Arabia, attacking and tying up smaller and weaker children—a theme that would resurface when he targeted the weaker elderly during his murder spree. During a school-sponsored swimming outing he had attempted to drown several classmates by holding their heads under the water until teachers were forced to intervene. He set fires at school and once pushed a classmate off of a moving bus. On another occasion he stabbed a teacher in the hand with a pair of scissors. In another event, a psychiatric nurse who tried to examine Erskine was taken hostage by him as he held a pair of scissors to her throat. He strangled the classroom guinea pig. Whenever any female staff tried to be empathetic and show him any type of affection he would expose his genitals or rub up against them.

There was frequent talk that Erskine demonstrated clear signs and symptoms of schizophrenia as a teenager but nothing ever came out of it. He never had therapy or medication or any real psychiatric evaluation.

By the time Erskine was 16 years of age he had turned to drugs and particularly enjoyed inhalants. This latest display of misbehavior was too much for his mother who eventually kicked him out of the house, forcing him to survive on his own. When Erskine tried to give his younger brother marijuana she finally disowned him. He never saw any of his family members ever again and was forced to spend the next seven years of his life "drifting through the twilight world of London's homeless and rootless" living in squats and hostels in Brixton and Stockwell and getting involved with petty crime which primarily took the shape of failed burglaries on primarily the elderly.

Erskine's violent tendencies continued to worsen.

When he was 18 he stabbed a young male with whom he was having a homosexual relationship at the time. Erskine had burst into his boyfriend's bedroom and stabbed and slashed at his body while he lay in bed. Whereas this may have been the first attack of someone in bed it was a glaring omen of the terror he would wreak in six years.

Erskine was described my many who knew him as a persistent loner who drifted through life and due to no direction of any type of social support system started a life of crime. Erskine was also a Rastafarian due to his Caribbean heritage but was shunned by fellow Rastafarians due to his habit of theft.

An unsuccessful burglar, he was jailed on many occasions.

Among Erskine's favorite "drugs" were solvents—such as glue—which he would inhale. Among the most oft-cited short term effects of huffing glue are hallucinations, delusions, and hostility. Long-term effects include depression, irritability, memory impairment, diminished intelligence, and serious and sometimes irreversible brain damage. There continues to be speculation as to whether Erskine was born with his psychopathic tendencies (nature) or whether his upbringing and environmental stimuli were to blame for his problems (nurture). The consensus is that a combination of factors worked together to create Erskine's sick and murderous persona.

Erskine subsequently spent considerable time in Borstals—youth detention centers—due to being apprehended following his many failed burglaries. While in one for burglary in 1982 Erskine would paint and draw pictures of elderly people in bed with gags in their mouths, with daggers in them, or burned to death. Additional pieces of "artwork" included headless figures with blood spurting out from their necks, people holding human hearts in their hands, disemboweled people, screaming faces, and copious pools of blood. Again, this was a chilling omen of what was to come. In one documentary about Kenneth Erskine and his crimes, one of his cellmates at Borstal, named James, described how horrific Erskine's paintings were and how he would frequently smile and laugh while painting them. As Erskine's only "friend" James became his confidant as well. The two would play chess to pass the time and then there were Erskine's disturbing paintings. James stated in an interview that Erskine always spoke very quietly—rarely above a whisper—and was very weird.

Borstal doctors were concerned enough to the point of asking the authorities not to ever free Erskine because they were seriously worried that he might try to replicate his paintings; however, he was, in fact, released and four years later he would begin his killing spree.

The Crimes

At some point Erskine decided to act out his fantasies and began to murder. He is classified as a geographically-stable serial killer who confined his murders to a specific area. As Erskine had no vehicle and roamed around the Stockwell area frequently confining his murders to this area was likely due to simple necessity.

The Stockwell section of South London is a favored place for the elderly to retire. In the summer of 1986, however, a serial killer conducted a reign of terror throughout the community that resulted in seven known deaths—and possibly another four—attributable to The Stockwell Strangler.

Eileen Nancy Emms, 78

Emms was a 78-year-old retired schoolteacher who lived in an "unkempt basement flat" on West Hill Road in Wandsworth. She was sexually assaulted and strangled by Erskine on 6 April 1986.

Emms' body was found on 9 April 1987 by her home help who, upon knocking on her bedroom door and receiving no response one morning, let herself in to find Emms in bed with the covers pulled up to her chin, seemingly asleep. There were no obvious marks upon her body. Initially, the cause of death was attributed to natural causes. The doctor called to the scene estimated that she died approximately three days earlier and signed a death certificate that stated natural causes.

Once the victim's home help noticed that her small portable television was missing, the police were called.

During her autopsy, the medical examiner revealed that Emms had been strangled by bare hands. There was heavy bruising to her chest which strongly suggested that her assailant had kneeled atop her while strangling her. Further examination revealed that she had been sodomized as the assailant had left semen around her anus.

A short Afro-Caribbean head hair was found on her sheet.

Janet Crockett, 67

Janet Crockett was Erskine's first July 1987 victim. She was chairwoman of her local tenant's association. Her body was found on 9 June in her flat in the Overton Estate in Stockwell. She had been strangled but, unlike Erskine's first victim—and subsequent ones—she was not sexually assaulted.

Police were able to immediately conclude that she had been murdered as she had considerable bruising on her chest due to sustaining two broken ribs as a result of someone kneeling on her while she was strangled to death. Additionally, her nightgown had been ripped from her body and folded neatly and placed upon a bedside chair.

Police also noticed that framed family photographs on the bedroom mantel had been placed face down or turned around. This action would be repeated at several of his crime scenes and speculation abounds as to what Erskine's underlying motive for doing this was. Some psychological experts have surmised that his anger at his own parents' rejection without a healthy outlet for his emotions led to an insane jealousy of normal family ties. Another hypothesis was that he felt ashamed at his actions and didn't want any "witnesses."

Police were able to find a smudged thumbprint on a displaced planter and a palm print on the bathroom window.

Pathologist Dr. Iain West conducted Crockett's autopsy and compared it to Emms. He concluded that their methods of strangulation were similar. He stated that with weaker elderly victims unconsciousness would occur within 30 second and death after approximately three minutes. While Crockett's and Emms' murders were similar—and that they were both elderly—police had nothing else to link the two victims.

Frederick Prentice, 73

In the early hours of 27 June, 73-year-old retired engineer Frederick Prentice was asleep in his council-run elderly people's home on Cedars Road in Clapham when he was awakened by the sounds of someone entering his bedroom. He saw a young man enter and Prentice turned on his bedside lamp and ordered the intruder to leave. Erskine then pounced atop the old man, placed his index finger to his own mouth as a threat for Prentice to be quiet, and then sat upon his chest where he alternated squeezing his windpipe powerfully, then relaxing his grip, and repeated this multiple times. Prentice told police that his assailant had whispered only one word over and over: "Kill." Prentice was able to push the alarm button near his bed which caused his assailant to leave.

After talking to Prentice the police were fairly confident that all of the victims thus far were, in fact, linked. A shoeprint found at the scene would also serve to connect this attack with some of the other murders.

Prentice would later identify Erskine in a lineup.

Valentine Gleim, 84, and Zbigniew Stabrawa, 94

The next day Erskine murdered 84-year-old World War II veteran Valentine Gleim and 94-year-old Polish immigrant Zbigniew Stabrawa in their adjoining rooms at Somerville Hastings House, an old folks' home on Stockwell Park Crescent. Both men had been manually strangled and sodomized.

The intruder had been seen by alert night duty staff but had vanished before the police arrived. Point of entry was, again, determined to be an open window. Staff were also able to see Erskine fleeing the scene and estimated his height at approximately five-feet-eight-inches with a slim frame so at least now investigators had a clue about their suspect.

Of particular concern in these two cases was the discovery of a used flannel towel and electric shaver which suggested that the murderer had calmly washed up and shaved after killing two people.

Approximately one hour prior to the double homicide an elderly woman in a Stockwell old folks' home was attacked while she was in bed by a man grabbing her arm. She fought off her assailant so vehemently that he had to run off. Her description of Erskine matched Prentice's.

William Carmen, 82

Two weeks after his previous double homicide, Erskine struck again by strangling and sexually assaulting 82-year-old widower William Carmen on 8 July. This time he threw a monkey wrench at detectives by murdering on the other side of the Thames river, in Islington, North London. Carmen was discovered dead in his bed in his flat on the Marques Estate by his daughter. As was the case with Erskine's other victims, Carmen was in bed with the covers pulled up neatly to his chin and had been sodomized.

This time there was clear evidence of ransacking and theft as approximately £400 of Carmen's savings was missing. Family photos were also placed face down or turned around.

William Downes, 74

On 20 July the body of 74-year-old William Downes was found by his son in his Holles House on Overton Road flat in Brixton; the same location where Erskine's second victim, Crockett, lived. He was naked and in bed with the covers pulled up to his chin, his eyes closed, and his arms folded across his chest—classic Erskine signature. Downes' son had reminded him to keep his windows locked firmly at night a few days ago so as not to fall victim to the Strangler but he failed to heed these instructions and point of entry was, again, determined to be through an unlocked window.

Downes had been strangled and sexually assaulted like the majority of Erskine's other victims. There were semen stains on the sheets.

Investigators lifted a palm print from the kitchen wall and another from the garden gate which were eventually matched to the prints found at Crockett's home. Finding the owner of these prints, however, was not as easy as the process is today. In 1986, while fingerprints were on file on computer discs at Scotland Yard, palm prints were not. Investigators had a stack of four million files; however, by concentrating on London-based burglars and petty thieves, they were able to compile a more workable load. They were subsequently able to match the prints to those Erskine, a small-time crook with an extensive rap sheet for burglary.

Unfortunately, the police did not know where to find Erskine and while they were looking he struck again, killing his final victim.

Florence Tisdall, 80

80-year-old partially blind and deaf Florence Tisdall was found in her apartment at Ranelagh Gardens near Putney Bridge on 24 July. The caretaker of the apartments noticed her walker in the communal corridor and knew something was wrong as Tisdall was unable to get around without it. He found her strangled, sexually assaulted, and with broken ribs as a result of her killer sitting atop her chest. She had spent the previous day watching the televised wedding of the Duke and Duchess of York—Prince Andrew and Sarah Ferguson—even having her own hair done especially for the big event. Tisdall had lived in an almost empty block of flats where she had resided for the past 60 years. A cat lady, she had left her windows open so the cats could come and go as they pleased and this is how Erskine got into her flat.

It was at this scene where Erskine made, perhaps, his biggest mistake. Detectives knew immediately that Tisdall had been murdered because she was found in her nightgown, tucked into bed with the covers up by her chin. In reality, however, Tisdall's neighbors who frequently checked on her because of her disabilities stated that she always slept atop the covers in the clothing she had been wearing that day. When Erskine undressed Tisdall to rape her, he attempted to cover up his misdeeds by making it look as though she went to bed as usual and died of natural causes. Family photos were also placed face down or turned around as was the case at the Crockett crime scene.

One of Tisdall's neighbors stated that she saw Erskine near the victim's flat shortly after the murder had occurred "looking disgusted with himself." Thinking this to be odd she promptly notified the police.

All of Erskine's victims were pensioners and in all but one case there was evidence of sexual assault that took the form of sodomy; however, investigators and forensic specialists cannot say whether it occurred before or after the victims' death.

Investigation and Arrest

After the Crockett murder, Scotland Yard's Serious Crimes Squad Detective Chief Superintendent Ken Thompson—a Scotsman with 26 years' experience—was put in charge of the case and given over 200 detectives to devote to the search for The Stockwell Strangler. Interestingly, Erskine was originally nicknamed "The Heatwave Killer" because the murders occurred during the summer; however, when the majority of his murders occurred in and around Stockwell this nickname was changed. Further, plainclothes officers would stand guard throughout the night wherever the elderly lived.

At the height of the investigation, as many as 350 law enforcement officers were on the Strangler case which included 150 detectives and senior officers from the C1 Murder Squad who worked out of five separate incident rooms throughout London which were linked to a special Home Office computer. This network was called HOLMUS and was used to prevent wasting time by cross checking paperwork which proved to be detrimental to the investigation for Peter Sutcliff, The Yorkshire Ripper. Other police officers set up fixed observation points in neighborhoods with a high population of elderly residents and instituted extra patrols.

A psychologist was enlisted to create a profile of the Strangler and to provide potential insight into his signature to determine whether he was attempting to cover his tracks or was fulfilling some bizarre fantasy. The suspect was determined to be suffering from gerontophilia; or a sexual attraction to the elderly and the complete opposite of its better known opposite, pedophilia. Speculation abounded as to whether the killer's sexual paraphilia was a result of some relationship problems with his grandparents. Additionally, as his victims were all selected at random, authorities could not link the victims together with the hopes of finding some commonality between them that would enable them to identify and apprehend the man responsible.

The suspect was classified as a process-focused serial killer. The majority of serial killers are of this type; the other being act-focused wherein their own psychological gratification from the kill itself is the underlying cause. Instead, process-focused killers achieve a hedonistic psychological "reward." These types frequently "get off" on the method of their kill and they enjoy the perverse sexual thrill that accompanies the act of killing. The literature identifies four types of process-focused serial killers: gain in which the killer kills for profit or personal gain; thrill in which the act of killing gives the killer a rush or a high; power in which the killer enjoys dominating and manipulating victims and while sex is usually involved it is primarily tertiary to the kill itself; and lust wherein murder is associated with sexual pleasure and this type of killer will commonly have sex while in the process or killing or may engage in necrophilia after death. As far as Erskine is concerned, he can be classified in multiple subtypes. First, since he did rob his victims and steal money he demonstrates some elements of the gain process-focused serial killer. Secondly, he did obtain a rush or high from killing his victims and, therefore, does demonstrate some elements of a thrill killer. This element is particularly salient when he was seen by a witness—who would later testify against him—getting sick on the sidewalk after his final kill near where his last victim was found. The act of his getting sick appears to be directly attributed to the thrill her received from killing and having sex with his victim. Finally, since Erskine likely sodomized his victims after he killed them his sexual fantasies were of a higher priority than is typically the case for power killers. Thus, he demonstrates elements more aligned with a lust killer.

Coupled with the fact that Erskine targeted the same type of people and that he engaged in specific rituals which were part of his signature makes Erskine a classic serial killer. His smaller size likely contributed to his choice of the elderly as his victims because in their weakened conditions he wouldn't have much trouble overpowering them.

The palm prints were the most damning evidence investigators had at that point; however, they only placed Erskine at two of the murder scenes. Despite similarities among all of the victims' crime scenes, the fact that Erskine wasn't cooperating with police required detectives to find other evidence. Investigators from Scotland Yard took the unusual step of distributing his Erskine's picture to the media to try to find more witnesses and potential leads by hopefully jog people's memories as to whether anyone may remember seeing him. Thompson also did something very uncommon; he appeared on television, appealing to Erskine to turn himself in.

After Tisdall's death the search for Erskine intensified even more than was already the case; however, being that he was a drifter with no permanent address or any real belongings to speak of they had to search through the hundreds of hostels and squats in South London. His life was so devoid of meaning and friends to help detectives find him.

Investigators got their big break when they realized that since the suspect was likely unemployed that he would be receiving social security and unemployment benefits. Upon further investigation they discovered that Erskine picked up his benefits on alternating Mondays from a Department of Health and Social Security office in Southwark, South London, and that he was due to collect his next check on 28 July. The building was placed under surveillance and when Erskine turned up, right on time, he was arrested and handcuffed without any struggle.

Whereas items and cash from the victims' homes were, in fact, missing, police did not believe that robbery was the driving motive in the homicides. There were neither signs of struggle nor any signs of forced entry. Police surmised that Erskine entered the flats through unsecured windows.

Forensic evidence linking the cases relied upon the fact that the victims were all murdered in similar ways: by the assailant kneeling on the victims' chests and then placing his left hand over their mouths and strangling them with his right hand. The semen collected at nearly all crime scenes suggested the same genetic fingerprint in that the same suspect was responsible for all of the sexual assaults. Additionally, there was a single hair found in Emms' flat, as well as matching shoeprints from three of the scenes.

A hairdresser informed investigators that Erskine had approached her wanting his head and pubic hair bleached. While she agreed to the former she refused the latter. Apparently, while he was sitting in the shop waiting for the bleach to take effect he self-applied the bleach to his pubic region and eyebrows, the latter resulting in his getting chemicals in his eyes and requiring assistance in washing it out.

When questioned by Detective Inspector Brian Jackson and other detectives, Erskine's responses indicated that the detectives' jobs were to be much more difficult than they thought. Erskine spent the majority of the interrogation giggling, staring out of the window or into the sky, or masturbating. After he was arrested, psychologists placed Erskine's mental age at 11 even though he was 24 at the time. He had first denied that he was, indeed, The Stockwell Strangler claiming instead to be a petty burglar who had no motive to kill anyone. After vehemently denying his culpability and blameworthiness in the string of murders and seeing that he wasn't getting anywhere, Erskine then changed his tune and said, "I don't remember killing anyone. I could have done it without knowing it. I am not sure if I did it." He also tried to blame the murders on a whispering female voice in his head. He once stated,

"It tries to think for me. It says it will kill me if it gets me," and, "It blanks things from my mind."

He was clearly disturbed but not a fool in any sense. In fact, when searched, detectives found ten bank and building society accounts that Erskine had opened to hide the proceeds of his crimes. During the three-month span of murders, he had deposited over £3,000; quite a large sum of money for someone who was unemployed. This included a £350 deposit into one of his accounts on the morning after the Carmen murder. It was evident at this point that Erskine was amassing profits from his burglaries while simultaneously collecting unemployment benefits. This demonstrated that whereas Erskine did suffer from some degree of mental retardation and likely some psychosexual paraphilia he was not stupid by any means. In fact, he told detectives that his motive was to achieve notoriety. He said, "I wanted to be famous ... I thought I would never get caught."

During a lineup—or identity parade as it is called in England—surviving victim Frederick Prentice was able to definitively identify Erskine. Another woman who had witnessed Erskine vomiting on the sidewalk near Putney Bridge a mere 200 yards from the scene of the final murder on the night in question also picked Erskine out of a lineup.

Trial and Conviction

Erskine's trial commenced at the Old Bailey on 12 January 1988. He pled not guilty to the charges of seven murders and the attempted murder of Prentice. During his trial he would stare out the window or down at his feet as was the case when he was interrogated. When details of the murders were brought up, Erskine would masturbate.

The jury heard him confess to the burglaries of the deceased victims; however, he claimed that someone else must have followed him and killed the individuals after he had left. Nobody was buying this story.

After an 18-day trial, the jury unanimously found him guilty on all eight counts and he was sentenced to seven life terms plus 12 years for attempted murder with a recommended minimum of 40 years; one of the heaviest penalties ever handed out in British legal history. However, diagnosis of schizophrenia and other mental illnesses pursuant to the Mental Health Act of 1983 led to a successful appeal of Erskine's murder charges which were eventually reduced to manslaughter. He is currently serving his time at the Broadmoor Hospital.

In addition to his seven known victims, the police suspected Erskine of four other murders for which he has never been charged due to insufficient evidence to prove that he was, in fact, the murderer.

John Jordan, 57

On 4 February 1986, 57-year-old John Jordan was found in his Josephine Avenue flat in Brixton strangled beside his bed.

Charles Quarrell, 73

73-year-old Charles Quarrell was found suffocated in his bed on King James Street in Suffolk on 6 May. He had two handkerchiefs stuffed into the back of his throat, effectively blocking his windpipe.

Wilfred Parkes, 70

70-year-old Wilfred Parkes was found on 28 May in his Stockwell flat, suffocated and in bed. A nearby pillow was presumed to have been the murder weapon.

Trevor Thomas, 75

On 12 July 75-year-old Trevor Thomas was found dead in the bath at his home on Barton Court, Clapham. As Thomas had been dead for quite a while there was inadequate forensic evidence for investigators to link his murder to the others; thus resulting in Erskine not being charged with his death even though Thomas was almost certainly one of his victims.

As mentioned, Erskine has never been charged with these additional deaths; however, police were so confident that Erskine murdered them that they effectively closed the book on all of these cases. There is also much speculation that he likely killed prior to his first known victim—such as was the case with Mr. Jordan—and that because of his choice of victims their deaths may have simply been attributed to natural causes.

Aftermath

There is not much more information on Erskine due to a lack of any detailed studies of him as is commonly the case with other serial killers where the literature is rife with speculation as to what influences led to the individual turning to serial murder. His only possessions were meager clothes and some books from the building society. Other than a post-arrest diagnosis of schizophrenia, the mind of Kenneth Erskine remains mostly shrouded in mystery. In fact, his mentally-disturbed state has worsened to the point where he has been told that he will never be released from Broadmoor Hospital.

Psychiatrists have never been able to fully penetrate his mind and discover what makes him tick. He clearly has a problem differentiating fantasy from reality and appears to be locked in his own childlike world. However, there is one incident that clearly demonstrates his understanding between right and wrong. On 23 February 1996, Erskine prevented the possible murder of Peter Sutcliffe, known as the "Yorkshire Ripper" by alerting guards while another inmate, Paul Wilson, attempted to strangle Sutcliffe with the flexible cord from a pair of stereo headphones. Erskine was able to restrain Wilson from inflicting further injury upon Sutcliffe until guards arrived.

Erskine found himself on the receiving end of an assault. On Christmas Eve in 1997 he was attacked by fellow inmate, 34-year-old Keith Hanger. Hanger was serving time for the 1992 shooting of his friend after having escaped from prison. He walked up to Erskine and squirted liquid from an aerosol can into his face before lighting it with a lighter. Erskine was taken to Frimley Park Hospital in Surrey, in agonizing pain and worried that he would lose his eyesight; however, his temporary blindness was just that—temporary.

Psychiatrists continue to attempt to probe Erskine's mind trying to uncover more and more of his psyche toward, perhaps, finding what makes him tick. Currently, he is unable to answer for his crimes, as demonstrated by the reduced sentence due to diminished capacity.

THE BOSTON STRANGLER

NATALIE MORTON

Albert DeSalvo, the infamous "Boston Strangler" is considered to be "America's first 'serial killer' of the modern era". He is responsible for as many as 13 women's murders in the Boston area between 14 June 1962 and 4 January 1964. Victims were as young as 19 and as old as 85. Whereas police did not believe that all of the murders were committed by the same person, the public was convinced that one person, dubbed "The Boston Strangler", was the sole suspect.

During the hunt for the Boston Strangler, police were also investigating two separate strings of rapes committed by the "Measuring Man" and, later, the "Green Man"; both of whom were, in fact, DeSalvo. He was arrested on 27 October 1964. At the time DeSalvo was not connected to the murders; however, likely due to his insatiable thirst for infamy and attention, he confessed that he was. He was sentenced to life in prison in January 1967, and was stabbed to death while in prison in November 1973.

There continue to be doubts as to whether DeSalvo was truly the Boston Strangler. In 2001, DNA evidence proved that the semen left in his last victim's body was not DeSalvo's. Thus, the cases of the Boston Strangler—as well as why DeSalvo was murdered and who committed it—continue to remain open.

Early Life

Albert Henry DeSalvo was born on 3 September 1931—the third of six children—in the poor town of Chelsea, Massachusetts, to Frank and Charlotte DeSalvo. The DeSalvo children, particularly Albert, had miserable childhoods. Frank was a violent alcoholic who would bring prostitutes home and have sex with them in front of his wife and children. On one occasion Frank broke his wife's fingers, one by one, by bending them backward and knocked out all of her teeth. Frank was also physically abusive with his children and allegedly once sold young Albert and two of his sisters as slaves to a farmer who paid $9.00 for all three of them.

The details of the following six months are unclear as DeSalvo never talked about it.

Not having any healthy relationship upon which to use as a model, DeSalvo desperately sought the love of women. He claims that he and his siblings experimented with sex acts as young as five years old and that he started having sex at age eight with girls and women, in addition to prostituting himself to homosexuals. During his adolescence, DeSalvo was exposed to graphic sexuality; from his father's activities with prostitutes to his neighbors who were very promiscuous and who DeSalvo watched whenever he could and this likely had a huge impact on his sexual development and resulting paraphilia.

DeSalvo started school at age six and due to several childhood illnesses missed much school which resulted in his failing second grade and being placed into special education classes when he was in fifth grade. He graduated junior high school at age 16 and that was the end of his formal education.

As a child, DeSalvo tortured animals—one of the triad factors common to serial killers and present in 36% of serial murderers in an FBI study—and as a young adolescent he committed shoplifting and thefts, common to 81% of serial killers in the same study. As a result, DeSalvo had many run-ins with the law.

He began working at the age of 12; performing odd jobs such as delivering flowers and shining shoes in an effort to make life easier for his siblings who he loved very much. In fact, despite the violence and brutality for which he would be later known, he was very docile with his family members; even when provoked.

At age 16 he worked in a Cape Cod motel as a dishwasher and, in his free time, would watch couples making out through windows. His first sexual aberration was as a voyeur.

At this time, on 12 November 1943, DeSalvo was arrested for the first time; for battery and robbery of a newspaper boy—over

$2.85. He did receive a suspended sentence from incarceration but was sent to the Lyman School for Boys the following month. His IQ was tested while there and was 93; low-average. He commented after his arrest that one "can learn about every form of sexual perversion" in reform school. After his parole in October 1944, he obtained employment as a delivery boy; however, in August 1946 he was returned to the Lyman School for stealing a car.

When he was released the second time, at the age of 17 and with nothing more than a junior high school diploma, DeSalvo joined the Army and worked as a military police officer. During his time in the military he had a reputation for being obsessively clean and a self-proclaimed ladies' man who bragged about his many affairs with officers' wives. While he was getting the sex he craved, he said he didn't have the love he also wanted. In Germany DeSalvo met and fell in love with a young woman named Irmgard and they married in 1949.

Irmgard often complained that her husband's libido was too high and she did not want to have sex with him as often as he wanted it. She was also distressed by DeSalvo's common practice of masturbating frequently, sometimes even after they had just had intimate relations. His sexual problems would increase when he, Irmgard, and their infant daughter—Judy, born in 1955—returned to the United States after DeSalvo was honorably discharged from the Army in 1956. Judy had been born with a congenital pelvic disorder that caused a deformity in her legs which kept them in a permanent frog-like position so she required special braces. DeSalvo would massage her little legs and would tie bows around her braces.

The family settled in Fort Dix, New Jersey, where, less than one year later, on 5 January 1955, he was accused of molesting a nine-year-old girl while her mother ran out for a quick grocery trip. DeSalvo was apprehended and charged with carnal abuse of a child and released on $1,000 bail; however all charges were dropped when the mother did not want to subject her young daughter to having to testify in court.

The family moved to Boston to get a fresh start. DeSalvo took whatever jobs he could find; at a shoe factory, a shipyard, and then settled into construction work.

In 1959, the DeSalvos had a son, Michael.

DeSalvo was very restless working odd jobs but his lack of experience or education precluded him from finding anything he would consider to be better. DeSalvo always had a lust for infamy and he was already headed down that pathway.

The "Measuring Man" and "Green Man" Rapes

DeSalvo's "career" as a sexual predator began in 1961 when he pretended to be a representative of a black-and-white modeling agency and approached young women telling them that he had to take their measurements to see if they would fit the clothing. He would tell them that he was authorized to give them each $10 for taking measurements; $15 for doing so with the women clad only in a bra and panties, and $25 if they were nude, which would facilitate his sweet-talking himself into their beds for sex. However, some women complained to the police of his unwelcomed and inappropriate touching.

At this time, DeSalvo was also perfecting his breaking and entering techniques and was arrested for burglary; however, much like his earlier crimes, he managed to receive suspended sentences. However, DeSalvo made a serious misstep when, on 16 March 1961, he was arrested for burglary and, in an effort to self-aggrandize himself, told the police about his measuring "scheme". As would be expected, DeSalvo was promptly arrested for breaking and entering, assault and battery, and lewdness and was faced—for the first time in his life—with a prison sentence. In exchange for a guilty plea to the first two charges, the prosecutor agreed to drop the lewdness charges.

DeSalvo served 11 months in prison and was released in April, 1962. When asked why he perpetrated his "pathetic charade" DeSalvo said that he was neither good-looking nor educated but "was able to put something over on high-class people" and that he was able to outsmart college kids.

The first Boston Strangler murder would occur a mere two months later.

In May 1964, after the Strangler struck for the last time, there was another string of rapes in Boston, courtesy of DeSalvo. In this, his latest scheme, he was dubbed the "Green Man" because he would wear a workman's green overalls in order to gain access into single women's apartments under the guise that he was there to fix a leak or check something allegedly broken or whatever. Once inside, he would bind and sometimes rape the women. Occasionally he would ejaculate prematurely after he bound them and would then apologize and loosen their bindings. On some occasions he would also apologize to his victims when tying them up, telling them he had to fulfill "the urge." He never killed anyone during this time. Four victims went to the police and, as luck would have it, one police officer remembered DeSalvo from his "Measuring Man" assaults.

When the murders surfaced, the city of Boston's residents were terrified not simply because there was a serial killer on the loose but that the victims were not prostitutes or vagrants or some other type of "unsavory" character but respectable, middle-aged or elderly women who were attacked in their own homes. Things worsened when the murderer began targeting young women too.

The Murders

Initially, the Boston Strangler targeted elderly or middle-aged women; however, by December 1962, he had turned his attention to younger women with two victims being in their 20s.

While the manhunt for the Strangler was going on, Boston women were gripped by tremendous fear. Dogs were adopted from shelters in record numbers and hardware stores quickly sold out of deadbolt locks. Because there was never any indication of forced entry, police could tell women to be extra aware; however, the killings continued.

Anna Siesers, 55

In the evening of 14 June 1962, 55-year-old Latvian seamstress Anna Siesers was preparing a quick after-dinner bath before getting ready for her son, Juris, to pick her up for a church memorial service. The petite divorcee looked younger than her age would indicate and had left Latvia over a decade earlier with her son and daughter, relocating to the Black Bay area of Boston on 77 Gainsborough Street.

There was a knock at her door.

When her son arrived an hour later and could not get his mother to answer the door, he forced the door open and found her lying dead on the bathroom floor with the belt from her housecoat tied around her neck.

Boston Police officers James Mellon and John Driscoll found Siesers in a "shockingly exposed position": outstretched, on her back, her blue taffeta housecoat completely open, in a grotesque position with her legs spread apart. Her head was a few feet from the open bathroom door and the cord from her housecoat knotted tightly around her neck with the ends tied into a bow. This bow would become a signature of the Boston Strangler and some speculate that it had something to do with the bows DeSalvo would tie on his daughter's leg braces. There were also signs that Siesers was sexually assaulted with some unknown object.

The murderer made it look as though he ransacked her apartment; however, nothing of value was taken.

At first, police believed that the crime likely began as a burglary and when he saw the victim in her housecoat he couldn't control himself, sexually assaulted her, and then killed her so he couldn't be identified.

This first murder was highly organized and proficient. DeSalvo confessed that he parked his car blocks away, wore gloves, disposed of his bloodied clothing quickly, and engaged in conversation with someone on the street as an alibi.

Mary Mullen, 85

On 28 June 1962, DeSalvo knocked on 85-year-old Mary Mullen's door under the guise that he was there to do some repairs on her apartment. Of particular interest was that most of his victims' apartments were of lower-rent and always in need of some type of repair so the residents had little reason to disbelieve anything that he told them.

'DeSalvo said that when she turned her back to him he put his arm around her neck and that she must have died quickly from a heart attack. He left her body on the sofa and investigators ruled her death as from natural causes until DeSalvo confessed to having a role in it years later.

Nina Nichols, 68

Just two days later on 30 June, at 1940 Commonwealth Avenue in Brighton, retired physiotherapist and widow Nina Nichols, 68, met her unfortunate fate at the hands of the Strangler. She was talking on the telephone to her sister when her door buzzer rang. Nichols told her sister—who also heard the buzzer—she would call her back soon but never did.

Like Siesers, Nichols' apartment had been ransacked but nothing was taken. She was found with her housecoat and slip pulled up to her waist and her legs were spread. Two of her own nylon stockings were tied tightly around her neck with the ends culminating in a bow. She had been sexually assaulted with a wine bottle and there was seminal fluid on her thighs.

Time of death was determined to be around 5:00 p.m.

Helen Blake, 65

That same day, 15 miles north of Boston in Lynn, Massachusetts, 65-year-old Helen Blake was strangled with one of her nylons and her bra had also been tied around her neck and fashioned into a bow.

She was discovered face-down on her bed, naked, with vaginal and anal lacerations but no sign of seminal fluid.

Nichols' apartment had been ransacked and nothing was taken except for the two diamond rings she had been wearing. The murderer had also unsuccessfully tried to open a metal strongbox and footlocker.

Ida Irga, 75

The next time the Strangler struck was nearly two months later on 21 August, with 75-year-old "shy and retiring widow" Ida Irga his latest victim. She was found dead two days later at her apartment at 7 Grove Avenue in Boston's West End. Up until-and including this time—there were no signs of forced entry, indicating that she had likely voluntarily let the murderer in.

Sergeant James McDonald described how he found Irga: on her back on the living room floor, clad in a light brown nightdress that was torn, thus exposing her body. A white pillowcase was knotted tightly around her neck and her legs were spread open with her feet propped upon individual chairs, facing the door so her displayed body was the first thing anyone saw when they entered her apartment. A bed pillow was placed under her buttocks. There was evidence of sexual assault but no spermatozoa were present.

The pillowcase had been tied so tightly that she had dried blood inside of her ears and around her mouth. This would be common with most of the Strangler's victims.

Jane Sullivan, 67

On 30 August, nurse Jane Sullivan, 67, was found, murdered, in her apartment at 435 Columbia Road in Dorchester. She had been dead approximately ten days before she was discovered.

Police found Sullivan "on her knees in her bathtub with her feet up over the back of the tub and head underneath the faucet." Her face was in about six inches of water and her bare buttocks were exposed. Her underwear was around her ankles and it was determined that she was killed in another room and then posed. She may have been sexually assaulted as there was a broom with bloodstains on its handle; however, her body was too badly decomposed that it could not be definitively determined whether she had been.

Again, there was neither sign of forcible entry nor was the apartment ransacked; however, Sullivan's purse was found open.

The city of Boston was gripped with fear and the Strangler wouldn't strike for three more months; thus, giving police the opportunity to investigate possible suspects.

Investigators claimed that the posing of the victims, the selection of apartments, and the use of household items with which to strangle the victims demonstrates a disorganized-personality serial killer; however, DeSalvo's ability to talk himself into his victims' apartments and his attention to not leave fingerprints by wearing gloves is characteristic of an organized-personality serial killer. Thus, DeSalvo was classified as the rare mixed-personality type of killer—one that was both organized and disorganized at the same time and a very difficult challenge for investigators. DeSalvo was about to make it even more perplexing for detectives.

Sophie Clark, 20

The next murder occurred on 5 December—DeSalvo's wedding anniversary—and it sent detectives reeling. After having strangled six women to death in two months, the Strangler stopped for four months. Some believe that his anniversary may have triggered him returning to action. Also troubling was that instead of being an older white woman, 20-year-old Sophie Clark—a popular student at the Carnegie Institute of Medical Technology—was a young, pretty black woman. Most sexual murderers do not cross racial lines, nor do they typically have victims of such diverse ages. This led to much speculation that there were two murderers at large in Boston at that time.

Clark was found by her two roommates with whom she shared an apartment at 315 Huntington Avenue; a few blocks from Anna Siesers' apartment. Clark had been writing a letter to her boyfriend when the Strangler struck.

Like the other victims, Clark was lying on the living room floor, nude with her legs spread wide apart, and three of her own nylon stockings knotted and tied tightly around her neck, along with her slip. Again, there was evidence of sexual assault; however, this time semen was found. There were signs that Clark struggled with her attacker and he had rummaged through her magazines and record collection.

In his confession, DeSalvo said he talked his way into her apartment with his usual repairman ruse and then told her that he was scouting for models and he would give her $20-30 per hour. When he asked her to turn around, he grabbed her from behind.

Clark's neighbor, Marcella Lulka told investigators that at approximately 2:20 p.m. that afternoon a man knocked on her door telling her that the super had sent him to talk to her about painting her apartment. After telling her that he would have to fix her bathroom ceiling, Lulka said that the man asked her if she had ever considered modeling because she had a nice figure. She put her finger to her lips and said that he became angry, almost as though he changed completely. When she informed him that her husband was asleep in the next room, she said that he said he had the wrong apartment and ran out.

She described him as between 25 and 30 years of age, of average height with honey-colored hair, and wearing a dark jacket and dark green pants. The super stated that he had not sent anyone to any of the units and this was approximately the time Clark was murdered.

Patricia Bissette, 23

The last of the Strangler's victims for the year was 23-year-old secretary Patricia Bissette who was murdered on New Year's Eve, three weeks after Sophie Clark. Bissette's boss went to her apartment that morning to pick her up for work but she did not answer her door. After he got to work and saw that she had never arrived, he went back to her place at 515 Park Drive in the Black Bay area; very close to where Anna Siesers and Sophie Clark lived. With the assistance of the building custodian, her boss climbed through a window.

Bissette was found face-up in bed with the covers pulled up to her chin. Underneath the covers, however, she had several stockings knotted and entwined with a blouse that was also knotted around her neck and tied in the signature Boston Strangler bow. There was evidence of recent sexual intercourse and some damage to her rectum. Of particular interest to investigators was that Bissette's legs were together and she had been covered which usually indicates guilt on the part of the perpetrator.

DeSalvo, in his confession, said, "She was so different. I didn't want to see her like that, naked and … She talked to me like a man, she treated me like a man." He said that he knocked on her door pretending to be looking for one of her upstairs neighbors whose name he had gotten from the downstairs mailboxes and she invited him inside to wait. She made coffee and they talked. He said that he didn't want to hurt her.

Bissette was in the early stages of pregnancy when she was killed.

Mary Brown, 69

On 9 March 1963, in Lawrence, Massachusetts—25 miles north of Boston—69-year-old Mary Brown was found beaten, raped, stabbed, and strangled to death after letting the murderer in believing he was there to fix her stove.

This time the murderer brought along a lead pipe which he used to bludgeon Brown about her head. He also stabbed a fork into her breast several times, leaving it embedded in her flesh. And also rather disturbingly, the assailant raped the victim after she was dead.

Beverly Samans, 23

On 6 May, pretty 23-year-old graduate student Beverly Samans missed choir practice at the Second Unitarian Church in Back Bay. A friend went to her apartment and unlocked her door with the spare key she had given him. The first thing he noticed was Samans lying on a sofa bed, her legs spread apart. Her hands were bound behind her back with one of her scarves and a stocking and two handkerchiefs were knotted together and tied around her neck. A cloth was places over her mouth that covered another cloth that had been stuffed into her mouth.

At first glance she appeared to have been strangled to death; however, the real cause of death was the four stab wounds to her throat. She had sustained an additional 18 stab wounds arranged in a bullseye pattern around her left breast. The ligature around her neck was not tied tightly enough to kill her. She had also been repeatedly raped. The bloody knife was found in her kitchen sink.

Her time of death was estimated at approximately 48 to 72 hours previously.

Because Samans was studying to be an opera singer there was speculation that her throat muscles were too developed and caused problems for the murder when he attempted to strangle her, thus resulting in his stabbing her to death.

Evelyn Corbin, 58

On 8 September, pretty 58-year-old divorcee Evelyn Corbin was found murdered in her apartment. She was lying face-up across the bed, nude, with her underwear stuffed into her mouth as a makeshift gag. It was determined that Corbin had been manually strangled and the killer left his trademark bow tied by a nylon around her ankle. There were several lipstick-marked tissues which contained trace amounts of seminal fluid. Spermatozoa were found in her mouth only.

Her apartment had been searched but nothing had been taken. Of particular interest was a lone, fresh doughnut outside her window on the fire escape that had not been put there by anyone in the building.

Joann Graff, 23

On 23 November 1963—the day after John F. Kennedy was assassinated and the entire nation was mourning his death—23-year-old conservative and religious industrial designer Joann Graff was raped and murdered in her ransacked Lawrence apartment by the Strangler. She had been strangled with two of her own nylon stockings which were tied tightly and in an elaborate bow around her neck. She had teeth marks on her breast and the outside of her vagina was lacerated and bloody.

The neighbor in an apartment in the building said he saw a young man in his mid- to late-20s with "pomaded hair" and dressed in dark green pants with a dark shirt and jacket knocking on the door of the unit across the corridor. The neighbor said that the stranger asked him if "Joan Graff" (mispronouncing her name) lived there. The neighbor told the man that she lived in the apartment below and then said that he heard the door below being opened and shut.

Ten minutes later, a friend tried to call Graff but there was no answer.

Mary Sullivan, 19

Sullivan would be the Strangler's last victim and also his most brutal murder. On 4 January 1964, she was found by her roommates atop her bed, naked, and propped against her headboard with her legs wide open, knees bent, and a broomstick handle inserted into her vagina. There was seminal fluid dripping from her mouth onto her breast and also seminal stains on the blanket. She had been manually strangled and a stocking and two print silk scarves were tied around her neck into a large bow. A cheery Happy New Year card was left by her body.

After this last Boston Strangler murder was committed, DeSalvo began another string of rapes; the "Green Man" ones.

Investigation and Arrest

Almost immediately after Sullivan's murder, Massachusetts Attorney General Edward Brooke took over the investigation and on 17 January 1964 he announced that the Boston Strangler cases was his top priority. Brooke created the Strangler Bureau that was headed by Assistant Attorney General John S. Bottomly; this choice much to the chagrin of Boston Police Commissioner Edmund McNamara. The team was comprised of Boston Police Detective Phillip Di Natale and Special Officer James Mellon, Metropolitan Police Officer Stephen Delaney, and State Police Detective Lieutenant Andrew Tuney.

A medical-psychiatric advisory committee was also created and headed by Dr. Donald Kenefick. The latter's first priority was to develop a criminal profile. They decided that the Strangler was at least 30 years old; neat, orderly, and punctual; works with his hands or has a hobby involving handiwork; probably single or divorced; would not come across as crazy to the casual observer; and has no close friends of either sex.

Several so-called experts had and continue to have conflicted opinions as to whether DeSalvo was, in fact, the Boston Strangler.

DeSalvo was arrested on 3 November 1964 after a "Green Man" victim identified him—the police remembered DeSalvo from his "Measuring Man" cases—and he was taken to the Bridgewater Mental Hospital.

Strangely, his wife was not surprised as she knew her husband was obsessed with sex and that one woman would never be enough for him. In fact, the "Green Man" assaulted four women in one day in different cities in Connecticut. He admitted to breaking into roughly 400 apartments and assaulting some 300 women; however, DeSalvo's propensity for exaggeration left investigators doubting as to whether this was an accurate number.

DeSalvo confessed to 13 murders as the Boston Strangler—two more than the police thought.

At Bridgewater, DeSalvo struck up a friendship with convicted murderer George Nassar who would play a pivotal role in this case. DeSalvo allegedly confessed to Nassar who is also among the suspects in the Strangler case. Nassar has been serving a life sentence for the 1967 shooting death of a gas station attendant in Andover, Massachusetts. His multiple attempts for appeal have been denied by the Massachusetts Supreme Court in 2008 and 2009, as well as his 2011 request for a writ of certiorari by the United States Supreme Court.

Former prison psychologist Dr. Ames Robey, who examined both DeSalvo and Nassar, called Nassar a "misogynistic, psychopathic killer and a far more likely suspect than DeSalvo" as the Boston Strangler, and he is not the only one with this opinion.

Some speculate that since DeSalvo was going to serve life in prison for his role in the "Green Man" attacks, the two colluded so Nassar could collect the reward money that the two men would split. Further, some speculate that DeSalvo's tremendous need for notoriety made him believe that his confession would make him world-famous and that he might get book and movie deals from his "story".

During a 1999 interview, however, Nassar denied his involvements in the Strangler murders and that the speculation had "killed his chances for parole".

It was Nassar, in fact, who brought F. Lee Bailey and DeSalvo together as Bailey was also Nassar's attorney.

At one point in his confession, DeSalvo admitted, "I would go home and watch what I had done on TV. Then I would cry like a baby."

There was no physical evidence tying DeSalvo to the murders; however, he did know a lot of specific details. Something that disturbed the police was that DeSalvo's misinformation grossly matched the misinformation in the newspapers as well. Even family members of the Boston Strangler's victims believe DeSalvo was not the Strangler. They point to his taped confession and asserted that even though police said he had to be the killer because he knew things that only the killer would know, in fact, he confessed to certain events that simply did not happen. Therefore, many still believe—to this day—that DeSalvo got his information from the real Boston Strangler while in prison. Even DeSalvo's brother, Richard, believes that his brother confessed to being the Boston Strangler because he knew he was going to prison for life and wanted to "cash in" on book and movie deals while fulfilling his desire for fame, even if that fame was infamy.

Trial and Conviction

In an attempt to prove DeSalvo insane in his rape cases F. Lee Bailey tried to get his client's confession admitted into evidence; however, a restraining order and the appointment of a legal guardian for DeSalvo led to his confession being recorded but not used as evidence in his trial. Consequently, after an eight-day trial, the jury—after only four hours—found DeSalvo not insane and guilty of the "Green Man" assaults.

DeSalvo was sentenced to life in prison on 9 January 1967.

Escape and Death

In January 1967, DeSalvo and two other inmates escaped from Bridgewater Hospital. DeSalvo had left a note on his bunk addressed to the superintendent stating that he had escaped to force attention upon the hospital's conditions and to protest his being sentenced to a prison instead of a mental hospital. With the Boston Strangler loose again, the city was once again sent into panic.

Police offered a $5,000 reward leading to information on the whereabouts of DeSalvo and his own attorney, Bailey, offered to double that reward if his client was caught unharmed.

The first thing DeSalvo did was go see his brother Richard who gave him clothes and a gun. He then went to Lynn, Massachusetts, where the police department was already on alert. Dressed in an old Navy uniform, DeSalvo went into a shoe store and told an employee he needed to use their telephone because he "had to call F. Lee" who then called the police. One employee asked DeSalvo if he was the Boston Strangler, to which he replied, "I honestly don't know. I know I did some of them."

DeSalvo was rearrested in Lynn, Massachusetts, and was transferred to the maximum-security prison in Walpole where he later recanted his confessions.

On 25 November 1973, at the age of 42, Albert DeSalvo was stabbed to death in the Walpole Prison's infirmary.

Of particular interest was that DeSalvo called Dr. Robey a mere 12 hours before his death saying that he wanted to "tell the real story" of the Boston Strangler.

DeSalvo wrote a poem while incarcerated, a couple of years before he was killed. It ends:

Today he sits in a prison cell,

Deep inside only a secret he can tell.

People everywhere are still in doubt,

Is the Strangler in prison or roaming about?

Both DeSalvo's murder case and that of the Boston Strangler remain open; the latter due to doubts that DeSalvo was, in fact, the real killer.

Aftermath

In 2001, George Washington University Professor of Forensic Evidence James Starrs asserted that DNA evidence found on Mary Sullivan's body did not match DeSalvo's DNA. The team of forensic scientists revealed that their tests discovered DNA from two individuals other than Sullivan and that DeSalvo was not one of them.

Sullivan's nephew Casey Sherman, a television producer who penned a book in 2003 entitled A Rose for Mary, has spent the past dozen or so years trying to prove that DeSalvo did not murder his aunt based upon the fact that DeSalvo "was convicted solely on the basis of a confession, which was riddled with inaccuracies." Sherman, like others, believes that DeSalvo, being faced with many years in prison, made up his confession with the hopes of procuring a book and movie deal so he could support his wife and children. Further, Sherman believes that DeSalvo was killed in prison because he was preparing to tell the real story, that his death was a "hit", and that prison officials were complicit. Sherman alleges that in order to get to DeSalvo, his murderer "had to go through six checkpoints, stab him 28 times, and then go back through those six checkpoints covered in blood."

DeSalvo's life was the subject of the 1968 film The Boston Strangler that starred Tony Curtis as DeSalvo, Henry Fonda and George Kennedy as the officers who apprehended him; however, the film was highly fictionalized, assuming that DeSalvo was, in fact, guilty and suffered from multiple personality disorder. Additionally, the Rolling Stones' 1969 song, "Midnight Rambler" has lyrics based upon DeSalvo.

TIMOTHY WILSON SPENCER

121

JEFF THOMAS

Timothy Wilson Spencer has the distinction of being the first American serial killer to be convicted on the basis of DNA evidence—evidence that also exonerated a man who had been in prison after being wrongly convicted of committing one of Spencer's murders. A troubled adolescent from Arlington, Virginia, with a deep hatred of women, Spencer utilized his cat-burglar skills, strength, and agility to gain entry into his victims' homes, lay wait, and then bind, rape, torture, and murder them. In total, Spencer had been linked to five murders and at least nine rapes in both Richmond and Arlington, Virginia. He was convicted of the murders of four of his victims and sentenced to death. Spencer was ultimately executed in the electric chair on 27 April 1994.

Early Life

Timothy Wilson Spencer was born on 17 March 1962 in Arlington, Virginia, and raised in the Green Valley section of town which was known as a lower-income, tough, predominately Black neighborhood. His parents were hard workers and had attended college but had divorced when he and his younger brother Travis were young. Travis commented that their mom was the best mother ever who worked hard to support them and spent time with them.

As an adolescent he had become increasing rebellious, first getting into trouble at the age of nine and again at 12 for urinating and defecating in the school yard. He was a poor student but intelligent. In the professional literature Spencer would be classified as a life-course-persistent offender who began deviant behavior at a young age which continued throughout his life with escalating degrees of crime. He had been implicated and/or convicted of six prior burglaries (three as a juvenile) and three counts of trespassing before being arrested for burglary in 1984 for which he served three years in prison before being released to a halfway house in the Southside area that was a transitional residence for nonviolent offenders. Because Spencer's conviction was for burglary he was considered to be nonviolent even though the evidence would ultimately show that he was a deliberately violent rapist and murderer. While in the halfway house Spencer was a loner who ate at the end of the table away from others and even watched television away from the rest of the residents. He did speak to one woman who worked at the halfway house and worked on her car so that he could borrow it. Whereas among the house rules were that residents sign in and out every time they come and go and had to follow a curfew, this procedure was poorly supervised and enforced.

In an interview, Spencer's younger brother Travis reiterated his utter disbelief that his brother was capable of what he did. Burglaries and other property crimes he said he could accept but someone who displayed such anger toward and hatred of women and who wanted to control them as badly as Spencer did by the systematic torture and strangulation of his victims was too much for him to believe. He even mentioned one time in his childhood where he and a friend stole some candy from a local store and were brought home in a police car that his older brother told him to never become like him.

A big question that has remained since Spencer's execution was whether someone like him was the product of nature or nurture. Some forensic psychologists say that deviant sexual preferences are hard-wired and that when combined with certain other factors can lead to deviant and aggressive behavior. The literature suggests that predatory psychopaths suffer from atrophy of the parts of the brain responsible for moral decision-making and aggression control and whereas this may be genetically influenced, the right combination of such traits coupled with environmental influences can make someone commit heinous acts. Spencer exhibited some of the "classic" signs of the serial killer typology—bedwetting, cruelty to animals, and a propensity for setting fires—which facilitated the escalation of his actions from breaking and entering to arson to burglary to rape to murder.

The Crimes

Debbie Davis

Spencer's first reported victim was 35-year old Debbie Dudley Davis. On 18 September 1987 he entered her home through a kitchen window with a rocking chair below it and bound, raped, tortured, and murdered her. Detective Ray Williams—who was dispatched to this and each subsequent murder scene in Richmond and stated that he had never seen such disturbing crime scenes in his entire career—remarked that the intruder had to have been exceptionally strong and agile.

The assailant utilized materials found on the premises to fashion his homemade ratchet strangulation contraption and this would be a commonality at all his subsequent crime scenes. In this case, he utilized socks, shoelaces, and a 16-inch vacuum cleaner extension hose.

There was very little forensic evidence at the scene—no hair or fibers—and no witnesses which suggested that the assailant was very meticulous. Except for the semen.

Autopsy results on Davis suggested that she was murdered between 9:00 p.m. on Saturday, 18 September and 9:30 a.m. on Sunday, 19 September. At the time of her murder, Spencer lived 2.7 miles from her apartment which would be approximately a 37-minute walk. The halfway house log showed that he left at 7:30 p.m. on Friday and returned at 12:30 a.m. Saturday. Davis had spoken to her parents on the phone from 8:30 p.m. to 9:00 p.m. that Saturday evening.

She had been strangled with a sock and vacuum cleaner hose that the Virginia court said had been "fashioned into a ligature and ratchet-type device." According to the medical examiner, the contraption had been twisted two or three times, ultimately causing Davis' death. The pressure of the ligature was so strong, in fact, that her neck muscles, larynx, and voice box were cut; blood was congested within her head; one of her eyes suffered a hemorrhage; and her nose and mouth were bruised. Her hands were bound by shoelaces and were attached to the neck ligature. It was posited that the more the victim struggled, the tighter the ligature became and that the suspect did this repeated times before finally killing her.

There were copious amounts of seminal fluid at the scene on Davis' nightgown and sheets, and vaginal and anal swabs demonstrated the presence of spermatozoa. The amount of semen suggested that the perpetrator repeatedly masturbated while alternatingly tightening and releasing the pressure of the ligature on Davis' neck. Two foreign hairs were found in the victim's pubic hair that were later identified through forensic analysis as being Negroid and, subsequently, consistent with Spencer's underarm hair. With respect to the semen, investigators discovered that the suspect was a secretor, defined as someone whose blood characteristics are found in other bodily fluids such as seminal fluid.

Analysis of Spencer's blood revealed him to be a Type O, enzyme grouping PGM type 1, PGM subtype 1+, peptidase A type 1. This particular configuration is shared by 13 percent of the population; however, specific characteristics of the analyzed DNA demonstrated that the sample would match only one in 705 million Black individuals. There are only approximately ten million adult Black males in the United States.

Dr. Susan Hellams

Two weeks' after Davis' death, on 2 October Spencer struck again when he beat, raped, tortured, and killed Dr. Susan Hellams. Hellams' husband discovered his wife's beaten partially-naked body on the floor of their closet. Point of access was discovered to be a second-story window that had a large portion of screen cut from it. Detective Williams commented that this was one of the most brutal murders he had ever seen.

The medical examiner identified the cause of death as ligature strangulation from two belts around her neck. Hellams also sustained a fractured nose, blunt force injury to her lower lip, a number of bruises and scrapes, and an injury consistent with a shoe on the back of her leg. Petechiae in her eyes suggested that she had been strangled and revived for at least 20 minutes before she was killed which suggested that the assailant was likely aroused by having complete control over his victim, not unlike the Davis case. Evidence of rape and sodomy included seminal fluid on her back and in the gluteal fold; small mucosal tears of the anus; and the presence of spermatozoa on vaginal, rectal, and perianal swabs. Additionally, an ample amount of seminal fluid was found on the victim's skirt and slip. Subsequent forensic and serologic examination determined that the seminal fluid and spermatozoa were consistent with Spencer's secretion type and could not have belonged to Hellams' husband. DNA analysis ultimately proved that the fluids were Spencer's.

After Hellams' murder, the unknown perpetrator was dubbed the "Southside Strangler" and the area went into panic mode over the term "serial killer." Panic ensued in Richmond; residents of the area left their lights on all the time, every deadbolt lock was purchased from stores, and even dogs from local animal shelters were adopted in record amounts. Police had told single women to nail their windows shut. A preliminary profile suggested that he was a white adult male, approximately 35 years old, a loner, intelligent, not a criminal beginner, and likely had considerable success as a cat burglar of sorts due to his agility and ability to enter residences without making a sound.

The police sought to find a connection between the victims to help identify a suspect. Nearby Cloverfield Mall in Chesterfield County proved to be that link. Davis had worked in a bookstore and Hellams had purchased books from her.

Diane Cho

Not long after, on 22 November, 15-year old high school student Diane Cho was bound, raped, and strangled to death. Cho lived less than a mile from the Cloverfield Mall and wanted to go to medical school. She was studying in her bedroom when Spencer entered through her bedroom window and overtook her so quickly that her parents and brother who were in the next room didn't hear a thing the entire time Spencer was assaulting and murdering her.

Spencer had carved the infinity symbol on Cho which, according to experts, signified his taking, keeping, and sealing the victim for himself since she was a virgin.

Cho lived very close to the Cloverfield Mall.

Susan Tucker

While on furlough from the halfway house in Arlington visiting his family for Thanksgiving, Spencer attacked Susan Tucker, 44, in the same fashion as his other victims on or about 27 November (her body wasn't discovered until 1 December). She was home alone at the time as her husband was away on a business trip. Spencer entered through a basement window and Davis was hog-tied with a rope, raped, and subsequently died from ligature strangulation. When her body was found she had been dead for a few days and those on the scene remarked that it was extremely disturbing and unsettling.

During her autopsy four-to-eight intact non-motile sperm were collected from vaginal swabs and DNA from semen stains were determined to have been left by a secretor. As mentioned, Spencer was that secretor.

Carol Hamm

Back on 25 January 1984, 32-year-old attorney Carolyn Hamm was raped, bound, and hanged in the door between her garage and house. Her body was found naked, face down, and her robe was on the living room floor alongside a piece of cord cut from a Venetian blind and a knife.

At the time, a McDonald's janitor, David Vasquez, was arrested and convicted of Hamm's murder after two witnesses placed him on her street that day. Despite police having doubt that Vasquez was guilty because of his less-than-70 IQ, he did confess and was, subsequently, serving a 35-year prison sentence. Authorities wondered if he had a partner who might still be at large.

Absent any leads at the time, Detective Horgas visited Vasquez at the Buckingham Correctional Center near the Blue Ridge Mountains on 7 December 1988. Vasquez seemed confused; he retracted his confession insisting that he couldn't have killed Hamm because he didn't drive and had no way to get to her house after work. He also denied having an accomplice. After the interview Horgas told the warden that he believed Vasquez to be innocent.

Other Crimes

Prior to Hamm's murder, there was a string of rapes between June 1983 and January 1984 in Arlington. Nine women had been attacked by a masked Black male in his 20s who carried a knife and broke into their homes via a window and who was dubbed the "black masked rapist." The last rape, in fact, occurred on the day Hamm's body was discovered. Detective Horgas wondered whether these rapes and Hamm's murder were connected. When he heard about the first two murders in Richmond, Horgas called Detective Williams to discuss the similarities between Horgas' rapes and the Hamm murder in Arlington and the two (at that time) murders in Richmond. Williams also mentioned a recent attack in Davis' and Hellams' neighborhood wherein a Black masked man had entered a woman's apartment through a window and was in the process of tying her up when neighbors came over to investigate noises and scared him away. Whereas Horgas was virtually convinced that the crimes in both Arlington and Richmond had been committed by the same person, Williams was skeptical due to the distance between the two cities and the fact that FBI profilers asserted that serial killers are almost always White.

Williams did tell Horgas that the Richmond police were trying DNA testing which, he said, identified an individual's unique genetic material that is found in every cell of a person's body and that they had already sent samples from the Davis and Hellams murders to Lifecodes, a New York State private laboratory that analyzed DNA for paternity tests. Prior to this, nobody in the United States had ever used DNA testing in a homicide investigation.

The Investigation

All of the murders shared overwhelmingly similar characteristics which demonstrated that the deceased were the victim of a serial killer with a particular signature that was unique to him. All of the victims were bound—wrists to neck—with handmade tourniquets fashioned from materials the killer found at the house through which he could repeatedly tighten and loosen the ligatures so that he could suffocate and revive the victims multiple times. There was substantial semen left at the crime scene near the body which suggested that the suspect likely masturbated while torturing his victims. None of the victims had defensive injuries which demonstrated that they were overcome quickly. All of the victims were White or Asian with a "stocky" build. All of the murders occurred on the weekend. Additionally, in every case the victims' bodies were laid crosswise on their beds (except for Hellams who was in her closet) representing submissiveness and in each case the victims' were "covered": Davis was redressed in shorts, a sheet was placed over Cho's buttocks, a blanket was placed over Tucker's buttocks, and Hellams' closet door was closed. Some experts have suggested that posing the bodies enabled the perpetrator to extend the crime scenes to make him feel even more powerful than he already did and that his covering them was like putting a lid on a trash can. The point of entry in every case was through a window in which glass was either broken or a screen was cut.

Detective Horgas was the first to overcome what is known as "linkage blindness" in which clues exist to link particular crimes but the Richmond investigators wore blinders as to how certain cases were, in fact, linked. One of the most glaring examples of this was that Richmond police were so intent on looking for a White suspect based upon their preliminary profile and, therefore, were initially against considering the possibility that the killer was, in fact, Black.

Horgas also reinterviewed the burglary and rape victims from Arlington prior to Hamm's murder. He discovered glaring similarities and a pattern of escalation that ultimately culminated with the perpetrator "graduating" to murder. Similarities included the fact that the point of entry was always through a window; lengths of Venetian blind cords had been cut and found near the crime scenes in multiple cases; and victims had been tied up, raped, and tortured. In some cases the victims' mouths were covered with duct tape (Cho's mouth was also taped). The fifth victim was locked in a car that was lit on fire but she was able to kick her way out and escape. Perhaps most damning was that the three-year break in between Hamm's death and the other four women's deaths correlated to the time that Spencer was in prison and that for every recent murder he had signed out of the halfway house; even seeking approval for a furlough to return to Arlington for the Thanksgiving holiday.

And then there was the DNA evidence. In addition to the samples from Richmond, Horgas hand-delivered samples from the Hamm and Tucker murders as well as some of the rapes to Lifecodes on 28 December 1988.

While waiting for the results, on 29 December FBI agents Stephen Mardigan and Judson Ray from the Behavioral Science Unit at Quantico went to Arlington to examine Horgas' evidence and ultimately agreed with his theory that the crimes in both cities had been committed by the same person. The profilers said that the key to all of the crimes was to reexamine the first rape in Arlington and that the perpetrator likely lived nearby because he would have wanted to commit his first assault where he felt comfortable such as in his own neighborhood. The agents also iterated that based upon their profile, this type of person would only stop if he were incarcerated of died. This spurred Horgas to look for a suspect who was arrested and incarcerated shortly after Hamm's murder in January 1984 and released just prior to the first Richmond murder in September 1987.

Spencer demonstrated classic signatures of an anger-retaliatory rapist-murderer who utilized sexualized violence against women who are perceived to have threatened or otherwise harmed the killer's self-image. Most of these perpetrators targeted victims usually in the same age range or older than the killer; however, in the case of Cho, despite being only 15 she looked older. Since he cannot kill the actual target of his anger he finds surrogate targets who he stalks prior to the assault. Spencer punished his victims for some wrongdoing by systematically degrading, humiliating, and incapacitating them.

The next day Horgas drove to South Oxford Street where the first victim was assaulted in a nearby wooded lot after being abducted from a phone booth at South Glebe Road and Second Street in June 1983. He racked his brain trying to remember who he may have arrested nearby during that time. He and his partner Mike Hill then went through over 300 files trying to recall. Four days later the name Timmy popped into his head. Horgas remembered investigating Timmy for burglary and arson of either a house or car. On 6 January 1988 Horgas remembered Timmy's last name: Spencer. Horgas conducted a driver's license check for Timothy Spencer and found that he resided in Richmond and that he had been arrested on 29 January 1984 for a burglary in Alexandria, Virginia, just four days after police discovered Hamm's body. After serving time in prison, Spencer was released to a halfway house in the Southside area on 4 September 1987—a mere two weeks before Davis was killed. Further, Spencer's mother lived less than a mile from both murder sites in Arlington and a mere 200 yards from the Oxford Street crime scene. Horgas said that it was like a puzzle wherein all the pieces fit together perfectly. On an interesting side note, had it not been for Horgas' memory he would never have found Spencer's name in any of the parole files through which he looked so diligently as convicts released to halfway houses were not technically considered paroled.

Spencer was placed under surveillance by the Richmond Police Department; however, after a week without him doing anything suspicious the surveillance was called off. This was much to the dismay of Arlington prosecutor Helen Fahey who—not unlike Tucker—was a single woman who lived alone in a rented townhouse far too similar to Tucker's home. She contacted Horgas and the two brainstormed ideas of how to get Spencer off the street before he struck again. Fahey suggested asking for a grand jury indictment which was considerably more difficult to challenge in court that an arrest warrant.

Arrest

On 20 January 1988 at 5:50 p.m. with his grand jury indictment in hand Horgas arrested Spencer at his Richmond halfway house on suspicion of burglary.

During the drive back to Arlington, Spencer was very tight-lipped, not volunteering any statements. Horgas knew that he needed either a confession or Spencer's consent to volunteer a blood sample. Horgas asked Spencer to submit to a blood test under the guise that it was necessary to compare to some blood found on a broken window in a burglary. Unaware of the advent of DNA analysis and that a blood test could be utilized to match a semen sample, Spencer agreed, to the delight and astonishment of Horgas.

On 16 March Horgas was notified that Spencer's DNA matched fluids left at the murders of Davis, Hellams, and Tucker, as well as one of the Arlington rapes four years earlier. Both Horgas and Fahey knew they had just caught a serial killer but Fahey had to convince a jury of Spencer's guilt based upon fledgling scientific evidence that she needed jurors to understand and accept in order to obtain a capital murder conviction. In fact, due to the relative infancy and lack of knowledge about DNA evidence, trial judge Benjamin Kendrick held a special hearing to determine whether the evidence was even legally admissible. After considerable inquiry Kendrick decided that the evidence was credible and would be admitted into trial.

Trials

On 11 July 1988 Spencer went on trial in Arlington for the murder of Susan Tucker. On 16 July after only six hours of jury deliberation, Spencer was found guilty of capital murder and sentenced to death. This was the first case in the United States in which a defendant was found guilty of capital murder and received the death penalty based upon DNA evidence; a noteworthy distinction, indeed.

Spencer's Richmond trials began in the Circuit Court of the City of Richmond, Manchester Courthouse on 17 January 1989 and ultimately, on 22 September 1989, he was found guilty of rape, burglary, sodomy, and capital murder and was unanimously sentenced to death following several unsuccessful appeals of his conviction and death sentence at both state and federal levels. It didn't help his case any that when the jury was shown crime scene photos Spencer was very eager to look at them as well; essentially wanting to revisit the excitement he experienced when he brutalized the victims. Aside from this display of enthusiasm Spencer demonstrated absolutely no remorse or other emotion.

In his first appeal with Supreme Court of Virginia, Spencer raised five issues: that the DNA evidence was unreliable; that his defense team was denied the opportunity to adequately defend against said evidence because the trial court denied a discovery request for Lifecodes' notes and memoranda, that the trial court refused to provide funds for an expert DNA witness for the defense, and that the prosecution failed to reveal any evidence of problems with Lifecodes' testing process; that the trial court wrongly admitted the DNA evidence; that the prosecution improperly removed a juror for alleged racially-motivated reasons in violation of Batson v. Kentucky, 476 U.S. 79 (1986); and that the attached aggravating factor of "future dangerousness" is unconstitutionally vague. The Court upheld the lower court's ruling. The United States Supreme Court denied certiorari.

On 10 September 1990 Spencer filed a petition for a writ of habeas corpus with the state trial court which was ultimately dismissed on 15 November that same year and subsequently affirmed by the Supreme Court of Virginia. Next, Spencer filed another habeas corpus petition in the United States District Court for the Eastern District of Virginia which was also denied. He then requested a Certificate of Probable Cause to appeal which was also denied by the United States Court of Appeals, Fourth Circuit. An additional Notice of Appeal and request for Certificates of Probable Cause were filed in district court on 29 April 1993 and 25 May 1993 which were met with the respondent's motion to dismiss. The Fourth Circuit Appellate Court granted Spencer's application for Probable Cause.

In this appeal Spencer's legal team raised seven issues: ineffective assistance of counsel at the original trial because they failed to obtain a defense DNA expert; that he is "actually innocent" of the crimes for which he received the death penalty and would not have been convicted had he been able to challenge the DNA evidence and if the "prejudicial injection of astronomical probability ratios" had not been introduced at trial; that his trial counsel were ineffective due to their failure to conduct voir dire on the subject of racial prejudice; that Virginia's proportionality review is unconstitutional and does not allow "rational exceptions"; that the jury instructions regarding mitigating evidence were constitutionally inadequate; that his trial counsel were ineffective due to their failure to present certain mitigating evidence; and that the DNA analysis was unreliable, should not have been admitted, and, thus, his trial counsel were ineffective with respect to this evidence.

The Fourth Circuit considered some of Spencer's issues. First, with respect to ineffective assistance of counsel, the court turned to Strickland v. Washington, 466 U.S. 668 (1984), in which the United States Supreme Court stated that in order to prevail on an ineffective assistance of counsel claim the petitioner must demonstrate that not only did counsel perform deficiently but that the petitioner suffered prejudice as a result. Both factors must be present and the burden of proof rests with the petitioner to prove whether there was a reasonable probability that if it were not for counsel's alleged errors the result of the trial would have been different and whether there was a reasonable probability that the sentence would have concluded that other mitigating evidence would not warrant death.

Spencer's claim of ineffective assistance of counsel because of their failure to provide a defense DNA expert was dismissed due to evidence that the court not only discussed with Spencer's counsel about procuring an expert but that because no experts interviewed were willing to testify on the defense's behalf does not make his counsel ineffective. Further, his attorneys had a blind DNA test run by an independent laboratory which corroborated the evidence against Spencer.

As to the voir dire allegation of racial bias, because of the publicity surrounding Spencer's first trial in Richmond, a change of venire—wherein a jury is selected and brought in from another county due to the fear that pretrial publicity would prevent the empaneling of an impartial jury—was granted and the jury was from Norfolk. The Court held that the change of venire eliminated race as an issue with which to be concerned and that it had no reason to believe that any prospective juror had any racial bias against Spencer and this allegation was also dismissed.

With respect to the mitigating evidence concerns, Spencer contended that had his counsel adequately investigated his background that they would have discovered that his school history, presentence report, and Department of Corrections reports all stated that he was troubled; that he was emotionally damaged by being erroneously told that his father was dead when, in fact, he was not; that he regularly ingested PCP; and that he may have some degree of organic brain damage and that his counsel failed to appoint a psychologist to evaluate his mental state. The Court said that the record reflected that Spencer's counsel did, in fact, conduct a thorough background investigation which yielded evidence that Spencer's attorneys in the Arlington trial had hired both a psychiatrist and psychologist who mutually found a complete lack of any mitigating circumstances and ceased any more investigation because of fear that more incriminating evidence might have been uncovered. In fact, per the recommendation of the Richmond criminal defense bar, Dr. Robert Mullaney conducted a pretrial evaluation of Spencer and Spencer's attorneys decided to not utilize Dr. Mullaney as a witness because the sole "plus"—Mullaney's opinion that Spencer's future dangerousness would be minimized if kept in prison—was far outweighed by the potential negatives which would ensue had Dr. Mullaney testified: these being the jury finding out that Spencer committed the offense, denied his guilt, and had shown no remorse whatsoever. Further, the defense counsel stated that if they had used Dr. Mullaney then the prosecution would have been entitled to have Spencer evaluated by its own expert.

As for Spencer's claim of defense counsel's deficiency in handling adequately DNA evidence, the Court argued that his counsel did, in fact, conduct a thorough investigation and contacted several experts, some of whom assisted throughout the trial but were unwilling to testify and, therefore, determined that counsel was not ineffective simply because they could not find an expert willing to testify. Further, regarding his "actual innocence" claim and that he would not have been convicted if the "prejudicial injection of astronomical probability ratios" into the trial record had not occurred, because a claim of "actual innocence" is not a constitutional claim then—and differs from a claim of "factual innocence"— the Court's discretion was limited. Ultimately, the Court held that Spencer failed to demonstrate any constitutional error that could have affected the jury's verdict. Further, the trial judge heard all of the information regarding DNA analysis including its statistics and limitations and still decided to admit the evidence into court.

Spencer's execution date was set for 26 August 1993.

Execution

Desperate last-minute appeals for a stay of execution were denied by the United States Supreme Court and Timothy Wilson Spencer was executed on 27 April 1994. He was pronounced dead at 11:13 p.m. He was 32 at the time of his death.

Virginia author and veteran detective Lee Lofland attended Spencer's execution and described, on his website, the atmosphere at the prison as "nothing short of surreal." He stated that Spencer entered on his own, calmly took a seat in the chair, and permitted the "death squad" to secure him and attach electrodes. His face was completely devoid of any sign of fear, regret, or sadness. When asked whether Spencer had any final words it appeared that he might say something but then stopped, silently. Lofland described how Spencer made eye contact with him and even made a two-thumbs-up gesture until the leather mask was placed over his head and he was executed.

On execution day, Davis' friend Lorna Wyckoff called Spencer a "monster" and the "personification of evil." Spencer's brother Travis said it was the most difficult day of his life, hugging his brother for the last time.

Post-Execution

Whereas DNA evidence proved critical for finding Spencer guilty, it was far more difficult procuring David Vasquez's exoneration since the samples from the Hamm murder were too degraded. Vasquez would need a pardon from the governor. Fahey formerly requested the assistance of FBI Special Agent John Douglas who had founded the Behavioral Science Unit in the early 1980s after interviewing some of the most notorious serial killers in history such as Ted Bundy, Charles Manson, and David Berkowitz, and identifying patterns in their behavior; their unique "signatures." Douglas' agreement to assist was the first time FBI profilers had ever been asked to prove a suspect's innocence.

Douglas said that one must look for a signature to link similar cases and that a signature was a type of ritual performed by a suspect that is truly unique. Douglas believed that the nature of how Spencer bound his victims constituted a distinctive signature in the five homicides and that use of ligatures and ropes exceeded the necessary amount of force necessary to control the victims was also part of his signature. On 4 January 1989 Vasquez was pardoned and became the first person exonerated, albeit indirectly, by DNA evidence.

Spencer's conviction was such a landmark case because it broadened the public and professional knowledge about DNA and that the jury understood its significance and was able to convict a serial killer of capital murder was a major revelation. The case also prompted Virginia to open the first state DNA laboratory in the United States in 1989 and to set up the first DNA database.

Shortly thereafter, in 1992, the Innocence Project came into being. A nonprofit founded by New York's Benjamin Cardozo School of Law, the Innocence Project has worked to free 179 of the 337 people exonerated by DNA evidence, including 20 who were on death row. The most common reason cited for wrongful convictions is erroneous eyewitness identification with mishandling of forensic evidence due to faulty tests and/or procedural errors the second reason. DNA is not completely infallible, however. The Innocence Project states that approximately four percent of those exonerated were originally convicted as a result of improperly conducted DNA tests which have prompted virtually all defense attorneys in criminal proceedings to request retesting on their clients' behalf.

In addition to Paul Mones' (1995) book Stalking Justice: The Dramatic True Story of the Detective Who First Used DNA

Testing to Catch a Serial Killer that focused upon Detective Horgas' efforts to link his cases in Arlington to those in Richmond and, ultimately, to Spencer, Spencer's case provided the basis for Patricia Cornwell's first crime novel Postmortem (1990) as she, at the time was employed as a computer analyst in the Richmond, Virginia's Office of the Chief Medical Examiner. Former FBI profiler John Douglas devoted chapter 11 of his 1996 memoir Journey into Darkness to Spencer. His case also inspired the forensic science documentary Medical Detectives which first aired on 31 October 1996.

THE SUFFOLK STRANGLER

141

JASMINE GREY

Steven Gerald James Wright was considered to be an ordinary, everyday English barman. Friends and family thought that his gambling addiction and his relationship issues were the brunt of his problems, but little did they know that was only scratching the surface of his nasty habits. He followed into the footsteps of the British serial killers that had come before him, like the legendary "Jack the Ripper", by primarily preying on the prostitutes of the red light district. Steven Wright is better known as "The Suffolk Strangler" or "The Ipswich Ripper" and he is currently serving a life imprisonment for the murders of five young women: Tania Nicol, 19-years-old; Gemma Rose Adams, 25-years-old; Anneli Sarah Alderton, 24-years-old; Annette Nicholls, 29-years-old; Paula Lucille Clennell, 24-years-old. All of these innocent women were murdered while working the corners of the red light district in Suffolk. The two-month-long murder spree received mass media attention and pushed the entire Suffolk area into utter panic. The heinous nature of the Suffolk Strangler's crimes, the mystery of his identity, the body count, and the mass hysteria pushed the police department into a full-scale investigation. After hard work, persistence, DNA evidence, and a few false leads, the police finally linked Steven Wright to the Ipswich Ripper.

Early Life

Steven Gerald James Wright was born on April 24, 1958, in Erpingham[1], a Norfolk village in the United Kingdom. His father Conrad was a military policeman and his mother Patricia was a veterinary nurse. As the second eldest of four children, with one older brother and two younger sisters, Wright claimed to live in an unhappy household. Patricia Wright divorced Conrad on the claims of domestic violence and abandoned the family when Steven was only 9-years-old.

After he was arrested for the murders of five women, Steven sent a letter to his father that suggested a childhood full of violence and anger that could explain his violent nature: "Dear Dad, this is a reply to your letter you are right you have never seen me angry before because I am a quite [quiet] and placid person whenever I get upset I tend to bury it deep inside which I suppose is not a healthy thing to do because the more I do that the more withdrawn I become because I have seen to [too] much anger and violence in my childhood to last anyone a lifetime. But what really makes me sad is the fact that I thought all the family feuds were behind me now I really thought we had made a step forward I just wish everyone would get along and work towards a family unit because all the bickering and point scoring against each other is really getting me down it seems you are pulling me one way and Pam is pulling me the other and in the end, something will give and it just seems to me that person will be me and that is the last thing that I want at the moment has I am sure you do as well because if I start to fall apart at the seams I don't think I could cope in here I need to be strong to cope with this nightmare like that but you said in the paper that when you looked into my eyes you would know whether I was guilty or not that really hurt me it was like a knife in the heart

---

1.   https://en.wikipedia.org/wiki/Erpingham

for you to even contemplate that I could even be capable of such a terrible crime."

Conrad Wright, his father, claims that he does not know what his son is talking about. He denies the abuse that Steven refers to and insists that he had a partially normal childhood. He was known to bottle up his anger and hyperventilate until he passed out. "He must be a raving lunatic," Conrad admitted after attending every trial in his son's defense. Conrad recalls his son during childhood as being quiet and introspective. Steven was also known to love horror films, Conrad explained later, "I was watching a film about a stranger and I thought how Steve loved horror films. He'd be jumping up and down, really into it."

Soon after he left school in 1974, Wright joined the Merchant Navy and became a chef on the ferries that sailed from Felixstowe, Suffolk. He developed a name for himself as a "ladies man" because he was always seen with women and rarely without a girlfriend. When Wright was only 20-years-old he met his first wife and the mother of his first child, Angela O'Donovan. They married soon after they met, in 1978, but the couple separated just ten years later, in 1987. This would start a pattern of failed relationships that would slowly chip away at Wright's mental stability. Wright would later make three suicide attempts after splitting with his wife and/or girlfriend.

After the divorce, Wright worked many odd jobs, including at QE2, where he soon used prostitutes to heal the pain from his recent split. Wright claims that this was when his indulgence with sex workers truly began; he would begin visiting specific parlors and ports whenever he "got the urge". He was working in the onboard shop on QE2 when he met a young stewardess named Diane Cassell. In August of 1987, Wright married Diane Cassell at Braintree register office. Not unlike his first marriage, his marriage to Diane did not turn out to be a happy one. Wright and Cassell's marriage was full of abuse and neglect. Elizabeth Roche, a former next-door neighbor, explains that abuse nature that Steven Wright did not attempt to hide from friends and family, "Steve used to strangle Diane right in front of us. He would pin her up against the wall and put both hands around her throat. There were, at least, three times when he did it in front of witnesses. It would end when either my ex-husband or I would pull him off or he would come to his senses." Steven Wright seemed to often portray sudden, violent mood swings and fits of aggression, Roche went on to explain her former neighbor, "He had an ability to have a violent row one minute and then have a calm conversation with you straight afterward as if nothing had happened. The only way I can describe it is to say he was a real Jekyll and Hyde character. He definitely had a psycho side to him." Due to their dysfunctional and violent relationship, Wright separated from his second wife nearly a year after their wedding date – they divorced in 1988. "The marriage was a nightmare," Diane Cassell later stated, "It was an awful time which I would rather forget. I was glad when it ended. It didn't even last a year and he went off with someone else."

In 1989, Wright was working at the White Horse pub in Chislehurst when he began his four-year-long relationship with Sarah Whiteley. They moved to Plumstead where they had a daughter in 1992. Sarah described Steven Wright as a kind, generous, loving father. While in Plumstead Wright managed the Rose and Crown Pub. Wright had finally managed to be in a stable environment for the first time in his life, but it didn't last very long. This all came crashing down when the weight of Wright's addictions became too much for him to control. Steven lost his job and his newly found family due to his heavy drinking and frivolous gambling. After he lost the pub, Steve moved back to Felixstowe, where he worked odd jobs, but never accumulated much wealth because of his spending habits. Most of his hard earned money went to prostitutes and sex workers.

It was pretty well known that Wright's mental condition was not very stable after his second split up. Wright drowned his emotional and financial issues with gambling, drinking, and engaging with prostitutes, which only increased the mountain of debt that was hanging over his head. Steven Wright tried to commit suicide for the first time in 1994, when he locked himself in his garage, in a running vehicle, in hopes of carbon monoxide poisoning. This attempt was a failure and he was pulled out of the car by police before it was too late. His family and loved ones were in shock. Steven's half-brother Keith Wright explained the reasoning behind his brother's brash actions, "He just got himself into so much debt. I suppose he couldn't find a way out." Wright's financial issues were increasing at a dramatic level, falling apart as he tried to fund his addictions. In an attempt to earn money, Steven Wright bought a £13,000 car on hire purchase then sold it. Simultaneously Wright continued to charge his credit card, creating huge bills and adding to the debt that would eventually get him arrested for stealing £80 from the cash register at work. Nearly £40,000 worth of debt was racked up before he fled to Thailand and declared himself bankrupt.

The most interesting part of Wright's life was the very short time that he spent in Thailand to run away from the debt he accumulated in England. In Thailand, Steven spent most of his time spending money on Thai prostitutes. Somchit Chomphusaeng was a Thai woman who claimed to marry him while he was hiding away in 1999. After their two week honeymoon, Wright flew back to Britain and never returned to see his wife again. She received a letter shortly after his departure from a woman who claimed to be his mother. The letter told Somchit Chomphusaeng that Wright had been murdered, or in more gruesome details, had been stabbed to death. She saw her husband again years after his untimely "death" when photographs of Wright were released from his arrest in Ipswich. Upon first seeing the photograph, his "widow" claimed that she fainted from pure shock. Later, when she was in the proper mindset, she explained her husband's deception: "It must be his ghost. I was told he'd been murdered."

A Life shared in Ipswich

Steven Wright met Pamela Wright in 2001 in Felixstowe, Suffolk. Their shared last name have no hereditary connection, but they immediately hit it off and Pamela stayed by his side throughout the guilty verdict of the murder trial. In 2004, Steven and Pamela moved into a rented apartment in the center of Ipswich, Suffolk, which was very popularly known as the red light district where sex workers sold their trade for anyone who had the money. Steven worked as a forklift driver on the docks of Suffolk as Pamela worked at a call center. Soon after the move, Pamela took up the night shift at her job, which gave her partner plenty of free time to indulge in his habits. The increased and late night hours made Steven and Pamela's sex life virtually nonexistent. His girlfriend was completely unaware that the change in their sex life, and the increased about of time that Steven would be alone, would result in the deaths of five innocent women. Wright now had the freedom visit local prostitutes any time that he "got the urge" and he took advantage of the situation. After Steven dropped his unsuspecting girlfriend off at work, he spent the late night hours prowling streets of the Ipswich red light district, which was where he captured and preyed on his victims.

Steven created quite a name for himself in Ipswich, as he frequently visited the girls in the red light district. He was nicknamed by the sex workers as the "Mondeo Man" because of the car that he drove, the "Silver-backed gorilla" because of his hair color, and the "Soldier" because he wore camouflage pants from time to time. Most of the women didn't feel comfortable engaging with him because of his out of the ordinary behavior. He was very unlike most of their clientele because he seemed too angry and he seemed to ask too many questions, claimed a former sex worker in a later documentary interview. Some of the sex workers went into vivid descriptions on how he would cruise the red light district dressed in high heels, a PVC skirt, and a wig, masquerading as a woman as he tried to pick up prostitutes. One Norwich worker explained from personal experience, "If you didn't get in the car he would get naked and just sit there with the headlights on. He freaked me out. The police knew about him." Her statement was proven right when Detective Chief Superintendent of the Ipswich murder investigation Stewart Gull stated that Wright was a pretty well-known curb crawler around this point in his life.

The Murders and the Investigation

Between the dates of October 30th and December 12th of 2006, Steven Wright murdered five sex workers from the Ipswich area. This string of murders took Suffolk by storm and sex workers everywhere were terrified that the Suffolk Strangler would pick them up next. These girls had few similarities despite their location, their occupation, and the drug habits that forced them to put themselves in an extremely vulnerable set of circumstances. All of these women were down on their luck and none of them were over the age of thirty when they made the fatal mistake of getting into the black Mondeo that belonged to Suffolk Strangler.

Tania Nicol was only 19-years-old when she encountered the Suffolk Strangler. On the freezing cold night of October 30th, 2006, the young girl left her home at eleven o'clock to service the curb crawlers of Ipswich's red light district. Sometime during that night, Tania willing stepped into Steven Wright's vehicle without hesitation, which hinted that Tania already knew him and did not expect anything unusual out of the situation, but when they pulled away from the curb the 19-year-old girl was never to be seen alive again. Usually, when Tania had a client she always made a point to keep her friends and colleagues updated on her whereabouts at all times. This night, however, Tania's friends did not receive the usual update. Tania didn't come home that night or any night after that. Tania's mother, who was unaware of her daughter's lifestyle at the time, reported the disappearance to the police 48 hours after she'd gone missing. The Suffolk police department regarded Tania as a high-risk target because of her profession and immediately took steps to discover her whereabouts. Detective Chief Superintendent Stewart Gull explained her disappearance in a documentary interview later, "She had literally disappeared off the face of the earth. Her phone record showed us a very flat line from the 1st of November. No incoming or outgoing movement of data at all..."

The Suffolk police had absolutely no leads to point them towards the missing girl, so they took to the public to find anyone who knew the whereabouts of Tania Nicol. Little did they know that while they were investigating the disappearance of one woman, another was in danger of falling into the same trap that caught Tania.

The name of the second victim was Gemma Rose Adams. Gemma was last seen on the night of November 14th when she boarded a train after visiting with her mother. She was only 25-years old. Much like Tania, Gemma always kept people updated on her location through texts and calls, but on that cold November night, the calls stopped coming. Her boyfriend, worried because Gemma wasn't answering his text messages, reported her disappearance on November 15th. The similarities between Gemma and Tania's profession, location, and disappearance, drew police to the conclusion that these cases were linked, and were most likely done by the same man, or same group of men. Upon this realization, the Suffolk police immediately stepped up their efforts to find the young girls and began to question random, passing motorists in the red light district for information on the girls' whereabouts. One of these random, passing motorists was actually Steve Wright. When he was stopped and questioned on his relationship with Tania Nicol and Gemma Adams, he claimed that he didn't know them. "We distributed some 20,000 leaflets around the area," Andy Henwood, an investigator, explained in an interview, "...we set up road checks at periodic times after the disappearances. We interviewed some 400 people in respect to Tania's disappearance and some 300 people in respect to Gemma's disappearance." Despite the efforts of the Suffolk police, they never received any leads to the whereabouts of these two missing women. As the weeks passed by, the investigators who had been hopeful to find the two girls were beginning to give up the notion that they were alive.

On the morning of the December 2nd, Gemma's body was found in a Hintlesham river by water bailiff, Trevor Saunders. "I noticed what I'd thought, at first, was a dummy, a mannequin. So I got down into the water to get it out," Saunders described his encounter with the body that he found upon checking the creek, "So I got down to pick it out, to clear the blockage, and when I got down to her, that when I realized that it [weren't] a dummy. It was a real body and I immediately thought to myself that I had found one of the missing girls." Due to the deposition of her body, Gemma's cause of death could not be established. She was naked when they discovered her, but there were no signs of sexual assault.

After Gemma's body was found, the police began a full-scale investigation to find the body of the assumed dead Tania Nicol. Despite the freezing cold temperatures, a team of divers swept through the disposition spot to find at least one strand of evidence. Less than a week later, Tania Nicol's naked body was discovered in a brook near Copdock Mill, less than two miles away from where Gemma's body was discovered. "Not in my wildest dreams did I anticipate that they would uncover the body of Tania Nicol," DCS Stewart Gull recalled, "We were no longer dealing with two missing persons. This was now a double murder inquiry."

A post mortem took place on both of the victims, but there were no concrete causes of death, due to the terrible shape of the bodies when they were discovered. It was obvious that the women died from lack of oxygen, but no tests could be made to find the culprit of the heinous crime. Ray Palmer, forensic scientist, explained the difficulty he had with retrieving evidence from the bodies, "...because it had been present in flowing water for a number of weeks, any prospect of recovering fibers or other debris for the skin, or any DNA from the skin, in that period of time was virtually zero."

The Suffolk Police department, which investigated an average of six murders per year, was not prepared for the two murders that took place in a matter of six days. The way that the bodies were disposed caused extra issues for investigators, "The bodies of Gemma Adams and Tania Nicol were found in fast flowing, very cold water, and the problem that presented from our perspective was because of the emersion of water, any trace evidence that was present was most likely to be destroyed or washed away." The Ipswich Ripper's choice of deposition location made investigators extremely wary about who they were dealing with, as they realized that they were dealing with a cold and calculating murderer. "The fact that he had placed the bodies in water so as to destroy any forensic evidence, suggested to me that this was a very, what criminologists would describe as an 'organized' killer. By 'organized' I mean that he carefully thought through how he's crucially going to avoid being detected by the police," explained criminologist, Prof. David Wilson.

Anneli Sarah Alderton was 24-years-old when she was last seen on the night of December 3rd. Her body was discovered just days after the first two victims, in a woodland near Amberfield School on December 10th. Alderton was the very first body to show up on dry land. She was found naked and sexually assaulted, but the most disturbing part of the scene was that her corpse was posed in a cruciform position. Unlike the other victims, Anneli Alderton's body had not been deposited in water, so it might've had traces of evidence that could actually lead investigators to the murderer. Forensic scientists immediately combed the scene for any shred of DNA they could find. Investigator Gull explained how he felt after the discovery of Alderton's body in an interview, "Once Anneli Alderton's body had been found, we were clearly into a different realm. It looked very much like we had a serial killer on our hands. It clearly had very obviously linked murder investigations in a very close area around Ipswich and all the indications of that stated that it was the work of one man, or men working together."

The discovery of three murder victims in less than a week lead criminologist, David Wilson, to the conclusion that they were dealing with a serial killer, "When the third body turned up I think I was the first person to say there is a serial killer on the loose in Ipswich and I think those words, I chose with a great deal of care because they were, as far as I was concerned, accurate and they also should've suggested, which I think they did, the gravity of the circumstances." Reporters all over the world flocked to Ipswich upon the news of three bodies. "What happened overnight as this crisis was developing was that the streets became filled with only one group of people and that group of people was journalists. Journalists seemed to be bumping into each other desperately hoping to find a prostitute that they could interview. "

Despite the fact that there was a serial killer in the area, targeting only prostitutes, business did not slow in Ipswich's red light district. Ipswich was a prominent area for drugs and the majority of prostitutes worked the streets so they could fund their drug addictions. This provided an ideal situation for the Suffolk Strangler. The police put out a clear message that warned all sex workers against putting themselves in a life threatening situation, but not many listened. All the working girls that were interviewed admitted that they were scared, but that did not stop them from working. These women had addictions to feed and bills to pay, and sadly, even a murderer wasn't enough to keep them away from the curb crawlers of the red light district.

"Is it my turn, tonight? Am I not going to come home tonight? But what choice have I got but to go out there?" Sarah, a woman who worked the streets of Ipswich, explains the terror that she experienced during this time, "Cars would come by and you'd be praying that they would pick you up to get money, but you're praying that they wouldn't because you don't want them to do what they're going to do." Paula Clennell, the Ipswich Ripper's final victim, was interviewed by an Anglia News reporter only a month before her body was discovered. Paula agreed that she was afraid of the disappearances, but she admitted that it was not enough to keep her away from the money that she desperately needed. "I need the money," She shrugged with her back turned to the camera. Paula Clennell died less than two months later, at the hands of the Suffolk Strangler.

Annette Nicholls was 29-years-old when her body was found on December 12. Nicholls was naked when she was discovered by investigators in the same woods that Anneli Alderton was found. Her corpse was posed in a cruciform position, just like Gemma Adams. Police searched the woodland overhead when an observer from the helicopter inspecting team, Maggie Williams, made another shocking discovery: the body of a 24-year-old Paula Lucille Clennell. A post mortem confirmed that Paula Clennell died from compression to the neck, but the cause of Annette's death could not be established.

After finding five murdered women in the matter of six weeks, DCS Stewart Gull reluctantly announced to the public that they were dealing with a full-fledged serial killer, "Although we only had the cause of death for two [women], in all probability they all died as a result of some form of interference with the airway. So you put all of that together and I think quite rightly, we drew the conclusion that we were looking for just one or more persons, who were involved together in the abduction and murder of all five women." Gull stated. The 600 officers and staff of the Suffolk police department were joined by 500 members from all over the country. It was the biggest manhunt that had ever been conducted in eastern England.

Media presence increased in this area tenfold, which eventually drew the attention of a very odd character named Tom Stephens. The 37-year-old man admitted in an interview with a newspaper that he personally knew all of the victims. It wasn't long after the interview when Tom was taken into custody. "The police had to arrest Tom Stephens on that occasion because he said, 'I knew all of these five women, they've all been back to my house, I do not have an alibi for the nights that they went missing," Explained Professor David Wilson, "In those circumstances the police would've been bonkers not to arrest somebody who is openly saying that."

Tiny amounts of DNA were retrieved from the bodies of Anneli Alderton, Annette Nicholls, and Paula Clennell. The DNA all link back to the same person Steve Wright. Wright used gloves in an attempt to keep all his crime scenes clean from his DNA, but he didn't consider the DNA sample that he left in Birmingham from his previous offenses. This sample sat in a national database until it matched the fibers that were found on the victims. Eventually, this forensic evidence released Tom Stephen's from custody and shined a light on the true Suffolk Strangler.

The Trial

After Wright was identified he was put under 24-hour investigation where the police followed his every move. Early in the morning on December 19th, the police arrested Steve Wright from his Ipswich home. When he was questioned by the police Wright refused to speak. Any questions would be answered with the phrase "no comment". During the first eight outs of interrogation, he recited that line over and over again. Even without a confession, the forensic evidence was enough to charge Steven Wright for the murders of all five women on December 21st, 2006.

Wright's trial began on January 16, 2008, at the Ipswich Crown Court. The only case in Wright's defense was the argument that Wright was a frequenter of prostitutes in this area, although he denied using prostitutes during the interrogation, which would explain why his DNA was found on three of the young girls' bodies. He focused on Tania Nichols, telling a story about how he picked her up with the intention to have sexual relations, but changed his mind and returned her back to the red light district. Again, this account differed from the one that he originally gave to investigators. On February 21, 2008, Steve Wright was charged as guilty on all five counts of murder after eight hours of deliberation. He received a life sentence without any chance of parole. On February 22, 2008, Wright was taken to prison, where he'll be forced to live out the rest of his years behind bars.

Wright is still alive to this day and he is having a terrible time in prison. His twisted state of mind after imprisonment is outlined in his letter to his father: "...I just wish everyone would get along and work towards a family unit because all the bickering and point scoring against each other is really getting me down it seems you are pulling me one way and pam is pulling me the other and in the end, something will give and it just seems to me that person will be me and that is the last thing that I want at the moment has I am sure you do as well because if I start to fall apart at the seams I don't think I could cope in here I need to be strong to cope with this nightmare like that but you said in the paper that when you looked [in] my eyes you would know whether I was guilty or not that really hurt me it was like a knife in the heart for you to even contemplate that I could even be capable of such a terrible crime. You say you want to help me the only way that will happen is if you make the effort to work together because all this he said she said you must understand is not doing my frame of mind any good I just want it to stop I do love you dad..."